YOU
CAN
FIND
ANYONE!

EUGENE FERRARO

Published By
Marathon Press
407 W. Santa Clara Avenue
Santa Ana, California 92706

ISBN 0-937309-05-2

Printed in the United States of America

To My Loving Wife Karin

TABLE OF CONTENTS

1.0 INTRODUCTION

Undoubtedly everyone at one time or another has found themselves looking for someone they could not seem to find. A distant relative a lost love, or just an old friend. What you probably found instead was that the task was a bit more complicated than you had first anticipated, and for good reasons. Like any skill or trade, proper tools are required. Without them, the job is difficult if not impossible. Locating someone is no different. Without the right tools you just can't do the job.

Over the years I began to realize how few people really knew how to find someone. Searching for missing persons for the most part was left to a select few who had "the tools of the trade". As a young investigator I found it difficult to learn because those with the knowledge were unwilling to share it. Even today I am occassionally surprised by someone who refuses to reveal a new found "source" or "secret" method. I for one feel somewhat different about the whole thing and as a result, chose to write this book.

What I am about to share with you are the methods and procedures used by professionals. I will reveal every source, method, technique, trick and bit of magic known to the trade. I will take you step by step from start to finish in a genuine investigation. And I will also show you, if you wish, how to make a little money at it. But most importantly, I will show you how you can find Anyone. With a bit of hard work, a little practice and a pinch of confidence I am sure you will find that special someone. Regardless of how much money you make, where you live, your age, sex or color, what you are about to read will change your life. For if you follow my instructions and use the tools

I am about to provide, You Can Find Anyone.

Best of luck.

Eugene Ferraro

2.0 WHO IS A MISSING PERSON?

Believe it or not, most missing persons are not actually missing at all. Frequently marriage, divorce, illness or a change of job cause people to move. As a result, contact with them is sometimes lost. Think about people you know and have not heard from in years. Haven't you simply lost touch with them? Are they really missing? More often than not these people do not even realize they are "missing," sometimes they're looking for old friends and relatives too. Considering this fact, our job of locating them will be much easier. Unlike people who do not want to be found, this group of people will have left us clues as to their whereabouts. Probably we know quite a bit about them even before we begin. For example, the location of their last known residence (an invaluable tool; we will see why later), names of children or relatives, hobbies, skills, health and so on. All this information points in the direction of our "subject." The trail will be fresh and usually clean.

Take for instance, a neighbor who has moved. What can you recall about them? Maybe you even have some old photographs. Do they still have a relative in town? Do they have any children? Were they possibly in college? Where? What year? Did you have any mutual friends? Where did they go on vacations? Did they have a family doctor? What was his/her name? Is he/she still in town?

Just in a matter of moments with thoughts like these, you could develop a good idea as to their location right now. Or with just a few phone calls, talk to them on the telephone.

11

Then there are the real missing persons. People or even groups of people, who have simply vanished. Every year close to 1,000,000 people across America are reported missing. Nearly every state, county, and city government has a missing "Persons File," and/or agencies searching for missing persons. The situation as of late, has reached such magnitude that State governments are now examining the feasibility of a national network to help locate these people. Washington has called the situation an epidemic and more than likely will fund such projects in the near future.

People become missing as a result of all kinds of circumstances. I think, however, the most terrifying is that of kidnapped children. Few things are as cruel, and the situation seems to be getting worse. Worse is the fact children under the age of five are virtually impossible to trace. Prevention seems to be the only answer. The movement aloft today to voluntarily finger-print all children is marvelous. Many cities and schools will finger-print children at no cost, and only the parents get a copy of the prints. If you have any children under the age of 18, I highly recommend you have them printed. It is a form of insurance anyone can afford and it could save a family untold anguish.

What I want to cover in this book, however, is the group of missing persons you can find. That group probably is around 90-99% of all reported and unreported missing persons. As we will see in the next section, the search quite often begins right in your own home. Let's get started.

3.0 WHERE TO BEGIN

The first thing that must be done in locating any missing person, is compile as much information on that individual as possible. To make the job somewhat easier and provide some organization to the task, I have developed what I call the "Subject Data Sheet" (see next page).

This data sheet is the foundation of your "investigation." If used properly, it will save you time and aggravation. Begin by filling in the blanks with the information you already have. This will indicate how much you know about the subject and how far your journey may be.

Obtain a manila folder and label it with your subject's name on the outside tab. Staple into the folder your subject data sheet, and all bits and pieces of paper you accumulate. Do not forget to attach a photograph of your subject, if available.

As new information is developed add it to your data sheet. Never fail to do this for it can be costly; we will see why this is so later on.

By the way, you are welcome to make or copy my data sheet for your own use.

SUBJECT DATA SHEET

SOURCE: _____ DATE STARTED: _____

DATE COMPLETED: _____

1. TYPE OF INVESTIGATION:

A. Missing Child: _____ _____

B. Missing Person: _____ Reported To Police:_____

Detective's Name: _____ Phone: _____

C. Credit Skip: _____ D. Birth Parent:_____

_____

2. SUBJECT:

1. Full Name: _____

                First   Middle   Last

2. Religion: _____ D.O.B. _____ SS#: _____

3. AKA: (Nick Name) _____

4. Address: _____ Phone: _____

5. City: _____ State: _____ Zip: _____

_____

3. DESCRIPTION:

Sex: _____ Race: _____ Height: _____ Weight: _____ Photo: ____

Color of Eyes:_____ Hair:_____ Marks, Scars, Tattoos:_____

Married: _____ Single: _____ Divorced: _____ Other: _____

Maiden Name: _____

_____

4. FORMER ADDRESSES:

Street: _____ City: _____ State: _____ Zip: _____

Street: _____ City: _____ State: _____ Zip: _____

Street: _____ City: _____ State: _____ Zip: _____

_____

5. Driver's License: _____ License #:_____ State:_____

Expiration Date: _____ /_____/_____

6. Auto: _____ Make: _____ Model: _____ Tag #: _____

State: _____ Own: _____ Buying: _____

Company: _____ Phone: _____

Address: _____ City: _____ State: _____ Zip: _____

Driver History: _____

_____

7. CHILDREN:

NAME: _____ DOB: _____

NAME: _____ DOB: _____

_____

8. SCHOOLS ATTENDED

Name: _____ Address: _____

City: _____ State: _____ Zip: _____

Name: _____ Address: _____

City: _____ State: _____ Zip: _____

_____

9. EMPLOYMENT:

Co: _____ Add: _____ Phone: _____

City: _____ State: _____ Zip: _____

Title: _____

Co: _____ Add: _____ Phone: _____

City: _____ State: _____ Zip: _____

Title: _____

_____

10. CHARGE ACCOUNTS:

A. _____ Acc # _____ C. _____ Acc # _____

B. _____ Acc # _____ D. _____ Acc # _____

_____

11. CREDIT CARDS:

A. _____ Acc # _____ C. _____ Acc # _____

B. _____ Acc # _____ D. _____ Acc # _____

12. BANKS:

A. _____ Acc # _____ Check. _____ Savings _____
B. _____ Acc # _____ Check. _____ Savings _____
C. _____ Acc # _____ Check. _____ Savings _____

13. PROFESSIONAL LICENSES:

A. _____
B. _____
C. _____

14. MEMBERSHIPS/CLUBS/ASSOCIATIONS/ETC.

A. Political Party: _____   C. _____
B. _____   D. _____

15. ARMED SERVICES:

Branch: _____ From: _____ To: _____ Rank/Rate: _____
Service No.: _____ Type of Discharge: _____

16. PERSONAL FRIENDS:

Name: _____ Add: _____ Phone: _____
City: _____ State: _____ Zip: _____

Name: _____ Add: _____ Phone: _____
City: _____ State: _____ Zip: _____

Name: _____ Add: _____ Phone: _____
City: _____ State: _____ Zip: _____

17. MAGAZINE SUBSCRIPTIONS:

A. _____   C. _____
B. _____   D. _____

18. HOBBIES

A. _____ C. _____

B. _____ D. _____

_____

19. HIS PARENTS:

Name: _____ Add: _____ Phone: _____

City: _____ State: _____ Zip: _____

HER PARENTS:

Name: _____ Add: _____ Phone: _____

City: _____ State: _____ Zip: _____

_____

20. CRIMINAL RECORD:

Offense: _____ DD #: _____ Date: _____

Location of Arrest: _____ Court Record: _____

3.1 THE DIRECTORY

Your next step is to locate a telephone directory covering the area in which the subject was last known to reside. If you do not have one, call your local library and ask where one could be found. Most central libraries have them. Look up your subject in all current and past directories available. Take notes and be sure to check all variations of the name and titles, if applicable. Check for spouses and children's names also. Use your phone and follow up all leads to the fullest. Do not be afraid to ask questions. If possible explain your situation, and ask for help. Most people will be very polite and happy to help a "Professional Investigator." Do not be afraid of wrong numbers, either. In some cases they may prove to be your only lead.

Some time ago in searching for a fellow with a very common name and not having a solid lead, I called every "Miller" in the phone book. (A simple task that took nearly fifteen hours.) Each person I spoke to I asked if he or she had heard from "Elizabeth," a ficticious name I simply chose to use. Surprisingly, no one claimed to know an "Elizabeth." A little hard to believe considering the number of Millers I spoke to. One gentleman, however, stated he had been receiving numerous phone calls asking for a Robert Miller. He said he could not understand it. The calls just started coming one day one right after another.

I asked the gentleman if he'd be so kind to refer the next several callers to my office, explaining that I would help them. He agreed and early the next day I received my first phone call. The caller was a collection agent hot on the trail of Robert Miller. The agency representative explained to me that Robert Miller was in fact Miles Roberts and that his date of birth was so and so, and he had resided last at so and so, and on and on. Using a trick explained in the next section, I then immediately located Mr. Miles Roberts. I received calls for Robert Miller for the next two weeks and by the time I received the last one, I had over six pages of information on Mr. Miles Roberts.

This story demonstrates two things. First, if you are on the run do not use the same phony telephone number more than once. Secondly, some of the most difficult cases can be solved without leaving the comforts of your own home.

While on the subject of the telephone, let's discuss the use of the pretext or "gag." A pretext is simply a "story" one employs when using the telephone in order to obtain information from the other party. For example: You have tracked your subject to an apartment complex but by the time you get there he/she has since moved, the neighbors have moved and the apartment has changed hands. You approach the new manager and explain your dilemma. What does he tell you? "Get lost! Our policy is not to reveal any information about current or past tenants!". Your only recourse short of a subpoena is to use a pretext.

Here's what to do.

Obtain a yellow page directory for that area and look up a camera shop near the apartment complex. Call the manager back (or have someone else do it for you) and tell him you are from the camera shop and are trying to locate old customers who have left unclaimed developed photographs. Explain you have some in the name of your subject, and they appear to be pictures of a Christening, a wedding, or some other special event for which someone would truly want the pictures. Explain also that your subject has not responded to his/her mail. If the manager does not at this point offer the information you desire, then ask for it. If you are told that no forwarding address was left, ask the manager to look at the subject's application or rental agreement and see if there is an address or telephone number of a relative you could "send the photos to." I use this gag repeatedly and it has yet to fail me.

I employ another pretext to obtain an address where I have only a telephone number. This situation, you will find, often occurs. What I do is call the number and offer something or state I have a delivery of some sort and need a current address. The item I use most often and with consistent success is a delivery of flowers. I use the name of a local florist and explain that my sales girl (whom I identify by name) failed to obtain an address for "this beautiful arrangement." The flowers of course have been paid for, and a small sealed card is attached. This pretext works especially well around holidays.

These are just a few examples. Use them, or think up some of your own. Be creative and be prepared to answer any questions if you are asked. Before you place the call think of and prepare an answer for every possible question you may be asked. You may only have one chance, so do not "blow it." Incidently, it is illegal to identify yourself as a police officer or an employee of any government agency. I would not resort to such tactics under any circumstances and neither should you. You could end up seriously regretting it.

Cross-street Directory

Another tool along the same lines is called the by-street or cross-street directory. They are simply reference books similar to the standard telephone directories, however they enable you to locate an address from a telephone number and a telephone number from an address.

The directories are a delightful tool but are a little expensive; about $350 a year for a single county. Additionally under normal circumstances you can not buy them, you must lease them.

In an office like mine, they are essential. Many companies and businesses in your community use them. Just find out who they are, and use theirs.

The first party to try should be the police. Not all stations have time for such services, but many do. Some fire departments also have them. Hospitals, ambulance services, credit companies, banks and even some libraries. If you have ever been in business for yourself, you know business to business favors are common. Do not be afraid to ask for help. Keep in mind these directories only list "listed" telephone numbers. For unlisted telephone numbers and addresses you will have to use a pretext. (This will be covered later.)

Haines, the largest of the cross-street directory publishers also provides a central locator library service called Address-A-Key and Tele-A-Key. By calling a subscription number, a Haines researcher will cross-street a telephone number or an address for you for a small charge. Write: Haines & Company, 1001 Derby, Winchester, Illinois.

City Directories

City directories are a great help. They are organized much like a telephone directory, however they contain the number of people in a family, their names, occupation of the primary bread-winner, colleges being attended if applicable, and how long the family has resided there. The largest publisher of such directories is R.L. Polk & Company, located at 2910 Clay Street, Richmond, Virginia 23230. Call them at (214) 631-8210. These directories are usually available at your local library. For additional help contact the Library of Congress; they have the largest known collection of current and past directories in the Country.

3.2 THE POST OFFICE

Your next stop is the Post Office. To perform this little known procedure, ask the clerk for an "Address Search Request Form" (the title may vary). This request plus one dollar will give you the subject's last known address. Three points to consider, however:

1. The name of the requestor will be kept on file and available to examination by your subject.

2. The information will only be available if the subject has filed a change of address card.

3. The post office is required to keep these cards for one year only.

The requested information is usually mailed to you, however do as I do. When approaching the clerk I always have a completed request form (see next page) and immediately hand it to him with a business card and the dollar bill. What you will have done is saved him time and demonstrated a slight degree of professionalism. I then politely request the information across the counter, stressing the "urgency" of the matter. This generally works and at the very least saves a few minutes if not days.

In the case of an individual who has moved frequently the procedure may have to be repeated several times.

On occasion, you may use it also to locate people who know how to locate your subject. For example, relatives, children, friends or neighbors.

The postal service will handle requests by mail, but be sure to use the proper completed form and to enclose a dollar.

For your convenience I have enclosed two types of forms. The first one belongs to the United States Postal Service. The second is mine. The format is different, but the information is essentially the same with one small difference. I have added the box and line stating "address unchanged/addressee has not moved." What I an trying to ask is, if no change of address is on file, is my subject still there? Most post offices will check this box for you if it applies even though they are not required to do so.

You may also try addressing an envelope to your subject, using their last known address, then beneath your correct return address write in bold red print, "Address Correction Requested 35-47, Do Not Foreward."

If the address is eventually provided it will cost you 25¢. I have had very poor luck with this approach, and frankly I rarely use it. Test it a few times and see if it works for you.

(YOUR NAME OR LETTERHEAD)

TO: POST MASTER
         (His Address)

FROM: YOUR NAME
         (Your Address)

RE: ADDRESS SEARCH

In Accordance with Section 262.7 of the U.S. Postal Service Manual, I Have Enclosed $1.00 and Request the Following:

☐ Forwarding Address/New Address

☐ Examination of Records

FOR: SUBJECT'S NAME
        (Subject's Last Known Address)

_____

Signature of Requestor

_____

POST OFFICE USE ONLY: PLEASE CHECK ONLY ONE BOX:

☐ New Address

☐ Address Unchanged / Addressee Has Not Moved

FREEDOM OF INFORMATION REQUEST

NAME AND ADDRESS OF REQUESTOR	FOR POST OFFICE USE ONLY		
	ACCOUNT 49299	$	
	FORM 3544	NO.	
	DATE	☐ APPROVED ☐ DENIED	INITIALS

TO:

In accordance with the rules and regulations of the U. S. Postal Service, request is hereby made for: *(Check one)*
☐ Examination ☐ Copy ☐ New Address *(Complete "Request for Change of Address Information" below)*
of the following postal record, if any: *(Identify as specifically as possible the record desired)*

REQUEST FOR CHANGE OF ADDRESS INFORMATION

LAST KNOWN ADDRESS *(Name, Street, City, State and ZIP Code)*	NEW ADDRESS *(Name, Street, City, State and ZIP Code)*

I understand that if the U. S. Postal Service does not have the record as requested above, it is not required to compile information. I further understand that the examination, copy, or request for last recorded change of address must be paid for in advance as prescribed in Section 262.7, Postal Service Manual, 39CFR 262.7; Federal Register 4774.

It is also understood that if I am permitted to examine the record, I shall not alter, falsify, cancel, destroy, mutilate, or remove any part thereof, under penalty of 18 USC 494 and 2071.

If denied access to the information requested, I understand that I may appeal to the General Counsel, Law Department, U. S. Postal Service, Washington, DC 20260.

SIGNATURE OF REQUESTOR	DATE

By law, businesses using a Post Office box are required to maintain a valid street address on file with the Postal Service. This street address will be provided just for the asking.

Private individuals using a Post Office box are ensured privacy. As a result the Post Office is not allowed to "give out" their resident address.

Should you run across a person maintaining a "box," you cannot "crack," try this approach:

Have an older or trustworthy looking person, your grandmother would be perfect,go to the post office and ask for the post master. Have your "friend" tell the post master "XYZ Company cheated me... I shouldn't have trusted those mail order people..." Instruct your friend to lead the post master into thinking that the subject is using his box for business purposes and hiding behind the protection afforded him by the law as a private party.

If done properly, this pretext never fails. I have had people at the post office tell me "Yeah, you are the third guy this week that has been ripped off by those dirty.......".

Most missing persons (about 90%) are found that easily. Imagine as a private investigator you could charge $150 - $250 for that simple service. Then again, you would probably have to charge the same to find the other 10%, a task that may take hours or even days. As I mentioned earlier, we are considering the broad group of missing persons; there are those who are, in fact, really missing or are playing "hard to find." (Obviously a postal search for someone who is dead would be a bit useless.) In the next section we'll locate the other 10%.

4.0 IT'S ON FILE

What about the other ten percent? The people that can not be found with the simple methods we have discussed so far. Your first step is to have some stationery and business cards printed. Order the minimum amount, but do not get the cheapest. I recommend the following be your imprint:

(YOUR NAME) RESEARCHER
HOME ADDRESS
TELEPHONE NUMBER

This title does not require a business license in most cities and affords you complete flexibility. Be sure to include your address and phone number.

While on the subject of business cards, let me quickly share a trade secret. Whenever the opportunity presents itself, snatch a fist full of someone elses' business cards (preferably without their knowledge). At first, collect any you can get your hands on. Then begin to become more selective. Business cards from television shows (i.e., "60 Minutes," and "20/20" types), real estate offices, banks, florists, and utility companies are the best to own. Why collect these cards, you ask? Because they afford you the opportunity to be anyone the cards say you are; at least long enough to accomplish your desired task.

Here is an example. Suppose your investigation has led you to an address where you need to identify the current occupants, or verify the name of the current occupant. Armed with business cards of a near-by real estate office, you could canvas the neighborhood asking just about any question possible with narry a second look. What type of questions would a real estate agent seeking a new listing ask you in your neighborhood?

You would probably answer any question he'd ask as long as you thought him to be genuine. What if someone bearing a business card from one of those one-hour television investigative magazine shows came knocking on your door. A clean-cut gentleman in a jacket and tie states he's been assigned to determine if the neighborhood is suitable for an upcoming news segment about life in America. He then asks for the names of your neighbors so he may contact them and you for interviews! Get the idea! I still keep in my briefcase no less than 200 different business cards. NOTE: Have several of each; can you see why?

Also, remember to look at the card before you hand it to someone and REMEMBER WHO YOU ARE! I have stupidly forgotten to do this several times, and usually at the very least walked away very embarassed.

Back to your own business cards and stationery for a moment. These tools are fairly essential. Invariably at some point you will meet someone who legitimately wants a business card of yours. Secondly, written correspondence on "business type" stationery is far more effective. Believe it or not, I have stationery for most of the business cards in my collection. An idea you might take up on. Go ahead with the expense and get yourself good tools.

Our next stop will be to visit the vast array of government files and records. If you know where to look and how to ask for it you will find information about anyone on file and in public records at some level of government. I break these sources down into six groups:

LOCAL
CITY
COUNTY
STATE
FEDERAL
NATIONAL

Some may also consider international sources, but for our purposes, they are out of the scope of this book. Let us now closely examine each catagory and the priceless information they can provide.

4.1 LOCAL

Once having covered all of the basics on a case and still finding myself short the information I need, I immediately start my search at the local level. These sources do not need to be followed up or developed in any special order. Each missing person is different so each case will be different. Start with the sources that best fit your particular situation.

Friends and Neighbors

Using a cross-street directory and the most recent address of the subject (if known of course), contact all of the surrounding neighbors. If possible go to the neighborhood and ask around. If you get a child on the telephone ask your questions anyway; remember that children are less inhibited than adults. Follow up on all leads. Run postal searches on the ex-neighbors if it is necessary to locate them. Take your Subject Information Sheet with you when you go out knocking on doors. Refer to it and try to fill in every blank.

Employers

Neighbors usually know where one another work. At the very least they know one another's occupation. Locate the employer. Sometimes a postal search is necessary here also. Locate a business just as you would a person.

When dealing with the employer be direct and up front. Should you suspect this will not work, tell them you are a process server with a subpoena for the subject and you desire his last known address, address of the next of kin or the address to which their final check was mailed. Follow up on all leads.

I also "gag" employers posing as another employer. The conversation may go like this:

ME: "Mrs. Stein, this is Gene Francis at Jetco Laboratories and we are conducting a pre-employment background investigation on Mr. _____ _____. Our records show that he worked for you between March 1979 and April 1982. Could you verify this please?" (Remember, most sharp personnel types will only verify information, or so they claim.)

STEIN: (After several moments of search) Yes, Mr. Francis, the dates are correct.

ME: (Now I throw in a bit about the job, performance and pay.)

STEIN: (She confirms some, corrects me a bit if I'm off.)

ME: (Next I "pitch" some story about his steady employment from late 1983 to the present, nonchalantly commenting how odd it was he had a period of "interrupted employment") ..."I'll be a son of a gun, I show no employment for nearly a year (stress year) after he left you. How odd?"

STEIN: "Gee wiz, I am surprised. He left us to join the XYZ Computor Company up in Santa Barbara. I wonder why he did not give you that information. You don't suppose they fired him, do you?"

Trade Unions and Associations

If your subject is a member of a union or an association, you have another excellent resource. Unions are brotherhoods. They collect dues and keep track of all of their members as do associations. I find the best approach here is to pretend your subject witnessed an accident and his statement is necessary to win a law suit for a fellow brother. Once again, I'd like to point out it is very illegal to represent yourself as an attorney or a police officer.

Also successful is a "pitch" in which you state you have a job opening available and since you owe the subject a considerable favor you desire to at least offer the position to him, before you put it up on the board of the Union hall.

Church Groups and Civic Organizations

These organizations can also be a wealth of information. Be creative, and follow up all leads.

Clubs and Teams

Same as above. Keep in mind these organizations collect dues and are constantly mailing correspondence to their members. They like to know where their members are!

Schools

Schools at one time were a cinch, but no longer. Even with colleges prospective employers often find it difficult to verify important information. Public schools are worse. Posing as a parent sometimes works, stating "The (new) school has not yet received the children's records." Then ask to be notified by mail when the records are sent. Use the first opportunity to ask "Now that you messed that up, I suppose you don't have our right address either! Come on, one more laugh. What address do you show?" Anxious to be right the unsuspecting individual usually will blurt out the family's new address (or forwarding address as the case may be.)

Also helpful, are alumni associations. "Planning a reunion," or "trying to find an old classmate" always works.

Post Office

If you suspect your subject owned a business which dealt with large quantities of mail (mail order, advertising, financing, real estate, etc.) go to the post office that served the area the business operated in. It is possible the business had a postage meter, bulk mailing permit, or business reply mail permit. If so, a look at the application for any of these services might be helpful. At the very least you will obtain what is known as a "street address" for the business, the name and signature of the authorizing officers of the company, telephone numbers and in some cases bank account numbers.

Should you find a business but learn it is a corporation (officer's names may not be contained in the information you found) fear not. Corporations are state regulated and information on them is public.

If interested, skip ahead to Section 4.5 and read about corporations.

Medical Records

Medical records are just about the toughest items for someone without authorization to obtain. They are very personal and well protected. But if you suspect a subject may have medical records somewhere, here are a couple of ways you can obtain information from them. First try calling the hospital you suspect has the records and ask for "Medical Records." One of their file clerks will usually answer. Identify yourself as an accounts receivable representative from a distant (varifiable) hospital. Tell the clerk your subject was treated at "your" hospital on such and such a date and has not yet paid. Of course *you* pulled his medical records at "your" hospital in order to develop a correct address for the subject. State that while searching the file you noticed he had been a patient of their hospital and you ask if you could compare addresses.

Note: Most hospitals file by last name and year admitted. Most do not have huge computers that will respond to the touch of a few keys, so you will have to narrow the field a bit as to not overtax the clerk and cause them to reject your request! I might add for a little authenticity, "Yeah, General shows the guy residing at 1632 East River Drive, (ficticious of course) but I checked that out too and he isn't there. I wonder if he owes you guys money too?" That should favorably arouse the interest of the clerk to the point of pulling the file.

Most hospitals will ask for the birthday or the Social Security number to positively identify a patient before they will answer any questions. So be prepared. If you do not have them, make them up. It will provide you the opportunity to ask more questions "to make sure *you* have the right patient."

Letters

Write a post card to everyone in the phone book who has the same last name as your subject. Code each card so you will know what addresses you have sent to should you get a response. State on the card something to the effect "Please contact Mr. _____ for an important message. Call (your telephone number)." Should anyone call you, immediately obtain their address and name. Even if they lie about the address, having coded your name you should be able to pinpoint the address.

The Trash Can

This source is often over-looked but very often the most valuable source. Somebody's garbage could be your key to success! Typically, people discard any items or "waste" they no longer have need for. Usually this is done with no regard for the information it may reveal. Bills, tax information, magazines, newspapers, trade journals, photographs, personal letters, business documents, receipts, collection notices and banking information are all things people throw away. Could someone learn anything about you if they sampled your trash for a week? Keep in mind, in most states trash is considered private property until it is placed or staged for removal. Trash day is the best day and will arouse the least amount of suspicion should you go **hunting**.

4.2 FILES AND RECORDS

City Business License

Cities issue business licenses. The filing and records office is usually located at the City Clerk's Office, in City Hall. Call first if you are unsure. With few exceptions, any business operating within a city's boundaries is required to have a business license. What you will be interested in is actually not the license, but the application for the license. It should contain:

A. Name of the business
B. Address of the business
C. The telephone number
D. The name(s) of the business' owner(s) or it's agent
E. Owner's address if not a corporation
F. Home telephone number
G. Type of business
H. Number of employees
 I. Filing fee paid
J. Date filed and the expiration date.

A copy of the application or computer printout containing the information is generally available for the asking. If your subject may be in business, and you have a good idea where, go to the city clerk's office and find out.

City Permits

Cities generally regulate all licensing within their boundaries. Such licenses and permits may include: dog licenses, bicycle licenses, parking permits, vending permits, parade permits, circus and carnival permits, fire permits, sign permits, fence permits, and of course building permits.

All of these permits will include the name and resident address of the individual applying. The appropriate offices are generally located in City Hall.

City Water

Cities generally regulate and administrate local water and trash removal operations. By using a telephone pretext (or going in person) you can obtain the name of any current or past resident using their services. Most agencies also maintain records of forwarding addresses for billing purposes. Their oifices are usually located near or in City Hall.

Also contained in the City Hall you might find other useful sources. Fire department, street and highway authorities, city parks and recreation department, city historical society and city planning usually all have offices in City Hall. Should you suspect your subject was (or still is) involved in any of these ask to have their name "indexed" and see what they have on file.

City Police

Though not too common anymore, some cities still have their own court system. All court decisions will be held as public information. So if the city in question has one, index your subject's name.

City Police are also sometimes helpful. Their accident and traffic records should be public and if so they are worth indexing.

Police also have available information and records which are not public. Should you know a policeman or know of someone who does, ask them for help. When dealing with the police, be upfront and *do not* pretext them. They are busy and if treated properly they could turn out to be the best friend you could ever have.

City Libraries

Libraries issue and maintain library cards. As a matter of practice they know where the card holders live. Most libraries consider this information non-public, and I question the legality of it, but in any case, if the proper pretext is used you can usually get the information desired.

The best is to go into the library, and request the file copy of "your" (the subject's) card, so you may correct the address to "your" new one. If offered to have the change done for you (librarians are so polite) then ask what address is shown on the card. State something to the effect:

"Gee, I wonder if I changed it (the address) last time.... no I did not, I bet it shows (make an address up).

The librarian will hopefully respond, "No, this card shows (your subject's address). You conclude the conversation with, "Oh dear, then I must have changed it last time!"

City Paper

Local papers may help you locate your subject by telling you exactly where they now live (via change of address card), or tell you enough about them so as to make your job a little easier. Most papers maintain what is called a morgue. A newspaper morgue contains all "dead" or back issues. Maintained like a library, a reasearcher can look up any subject or anybody, and if ever mentioned in one of the paper's issues, it can be located. Papers usually do not allow the public into their files, but most offer the service for a small fee. If the desired information is located, you are either provided an actual copy of that day's issue or a photocopy of the article or story.

Some large city papers maintain the same system for other papers, not just their own, allowing their reporters terrific pools of information and photographs.

Remember also, newspapers publish obituaries as well as important legal notices. Classified sections also sometimes contain ads for garage sales and moving sales. If in doubt check it out.

QUESTIONS AND ANSWERS

QUESTION: Why all the big deal about business licenses and fictitious names? How do I know my subject is in business; besides if I knew that I'd undoubtedly know where to find them?

> **ANSWER:** Hopefully, we know something about our subject. Possibly they have been in business before. Maybe a member of their family or a friend has been in business.
>
> A DMV report may show the subject owns a fleet of vans or dump trucks. Such information is highly indicitive that they may be involved in some sort of business.
>
> Additionally, statistics show Americans move at an average of roughly once every three years. So if your subject has had a restaurant in New York and you determined he is now somewhere in San Francisco, chances are good he is back in the restaurant business.
>
> What's more, most Americans (more than 50%) at some time in their lives try their hand at a business of their own. Have you?

QUESTION: How accurate is the information in these records, and what if none of it checks out?

> **ANSWER:** Good and great. The applicant usually has honest intentions when business license and fictitious name filings are made. It is only after the venture turns sour does the "businessman" start to cover his tracks.
>
> Secondly, if all the information does not check out, you still have learned two important things:
>
> 1. They more than likely lived in the county at the time of the filing.
>
> 2. They filed under other than normal circumstances, in that they attempted to hide something or someone. Chances are that there are others looking for them also.

4.3 COUNTY RECORDS AND FILES

County courts are probably the single most valuable source of information available to you. The "Courts" are usually broken down into jurisdictions, and I recommend you index every one of them for best results.

Superior Court

Superior court has two divisions: Criminal and Civil. Superior Criminal handles all felonies, while Superior-Civil handles all civil matters, usually involving $10,000 to $15,000 or more (each state is different).

Municipal Court

Municipal also has two division, criminal and civil. Criminal handles misdemeanors and Civil handles all civil matters involving sums less than the lower limit set by Superior.

Small Claims

Small claims is a civil court designed to handle all minor civil matters usually involving less than several hundred dollars (some states go as high as $2,500.00). Attorneys are not usually permitted in small claims court. The plaintiff (the one taking action) and the defendant (the one defending the action) must represent themselves.

Many counties also have Probate, Traffic and Divorce courts. Go to your nearest County Court house and find out what courts they hold. Regardless of the type of court, every court keeps detailed records. All of the records are public with only three (3) exceptions.

A. Adoption records - Most states **seal** adoption records. Only through a court order can they be **opened**. (See chapter on adoption records).

B. Criminal cases involving **protected witnesses**.

C. Criminal cases in which the accused was a minor.

Fortunately for us, these exceptions constitute only a small percentage of all court records. Court Records or **case files** contain every detail of the case and the people involved in them. Divorce records contain just about everything imaginable about the two people involved (sometimes you are even able to find out how often they made love!).

Court records are usually indexed by the names of the parties involved and the year filed. Good court houses file by year, plaintiff name and defendant name. So with the name of your subject you can index it year to year, as far back as you please. This sounds time consuming, however many courts now have their records available on microfiche, indexed by blocks of 10 or 25 years. This of course, enables you to search a name in minutes.

Should you find a case under your subject's name (ensure same middle initial) copy the case number, give it to the clerk and request the file. They will obtain it on the spot and give it directly to you. You will have to sign for it and are not permitted to remove it from their office. Most record offices supply desks and chairs for you to use. The larger ones even provide typewriters and telephones.

In reading the file skip over the legal mumbo-jumbo and just key off names, places, addresses and dates. Once you locate something of interest, read a page or so. Some files are very large (the IBM anti-trust case was over 100,000,000 pages!), so read only what is necessary and go on to the next file.

Should you not find a case in your subject's name, index other family members, friends or neighbors. If you cannot locate your subject, locate someone who can!

I have not mentioned anything about Probate court, partly because Probate court primarily involves those who are dead. Probate is the condition of an estate. Or more clearly put, probate is where one's earthly belongings will go if one dies without (sometimes with) a will. Sounds like a great place to develop information and probably is; I just never seem to have much luck there. The files include such things as property, addresses, names, businesses, amount of money and the names and addresses of the deceased's next of kin. So should you suspect your subject is involved in a probate battle, State vs. Them (states want their share, you know), index the Probate files. These files are particularly helpful when searching for birth parents or tracing family roots.

Grantee/Grantor

Your next best source of quality information is Grantee/Grantor. These records are located near the Court House at the County seat. They contain records of all real property exchanged, deeds, trust deeds, ground liens, power of attorney exchanges, judgements and any other type of **deal** two or more people can make and record on paper.

These records are indexed by year and party name. Each entry is given a file number or "document number." Should you find your subject's name on file, have the document pulled and examine it. Determine what information is useful and record it. Most commonly recorded here is the exchange of property; the sale of a house for example. Again, do not become overwhelmed by the legalees. Concentrate on the information about your subject. Also index the next of kin and other family members. Sneaky people (or those who are bankrupt) often buy and sell property in the names of their children. This action, however, involves the use of a power of attorney (simply one person giving their lawful rights to another), which will also be recorded.

Addresses, full names, birthdates, children's names, occupations and personal financial information can all be found here.

Property Taxes

Though usually admistered at a state level, records are maintained on a local level. Tax records on homes, businesses, real estate, airplanes, boats and ships are all found here. Such "real property" must be appraised and taxed on a regular basis (usually annually) These records are public and contain full descriptions and details of the property and owner, typically indexed by name and year.

Voter's Registrar Office

Records of all those registered to vote are kept on a county level. These public records include the name of the voter, addresses, occupation, birthdate, sometimes their Social Security Number, and of course their political party affiliation. These records are indexed by name (not political party) and usually are stored on microfiche. Copies of the voter's application card are available for the asking.

This source is continually updated, and is most accurate in a presidential election year; remember, one must register to vote!

Vital Statistics

Vital statistics are usually found in or near county courthouses. These records include documentation of all births and deaths within the county. A copy of the actual document is abailable to the public for a small fee.

Also available from the coroner's office are autopsy reports. These reports are usually held public, but afford no more information than the death certificate. Sometimes, however, the death certificate contains the names of the deceased's next of kin. Always provided are the parents, address and a full description of the deceased.

Birth certificates, of course, contain the full names of the parents, description at birth, date, time of birth and sometimes (recently) a Social Security number!

Also available on the county level are marriage licenses. If public the details of the marriage are yours for the asking. However, sometimes marriages are **sealed** and the information you may want will not be available for it has been held "**not for public view**."

Should you desire the search be done for you, or the search has taken you out of state, use one of the following agencies. Each should be able to provide birth, death and marriage information. If not, they will be able to put you in touch with the person/agency who can. When you do write do not hesitate to include a check for the fee and your telephone number. Many "nicer" government offices will help by calling you and providing the information you are seeking. As a general rule I telephone first. The cost of the phone call is usually less than the fee and the information is yours immediately. If they will not do a phone search and look up the information while you are on hold, then write to them.

ALABAMA $5.00
State Department of Public Health
Montgomery 36130

ALASKA $3.00
Department of Health and Welfare
Pouch H, Juneau 99801

ARIZONA $3.00
State Department of Health, P.0. Box 3887
Phoenix 85030

ARKANSAS $3.00
State Department of Health
Little Rock 72201

CALIFORNIA $3.00
State Department of Public Health, 410 N. Street
Sacramento 95814

COLORADO $2.00
Colorado Department of Health
Denver 80220

CONNECTICUT $3.00
State Department of Health, 79 Elm Street
Hartford 06115

DELAWARE $2.50
State Department of Health and Social Services
Dover 19901

DISTRICT OF COLUMBIA $1.00
D.C. Department of Human Resources
Vital Records Section,
Washington 20004

FLORIDA $2.00
State Division of Health, P.0. Box 210
Jacksonville 32201

GEORGIA $3.00
Department of Human Resources
Vital Records Section
Atlanta 30334

HAWAII $2.00
State Department of Health, P.0. Box 3378
Honolulu 96801

IDAHO $2.00
Bureau of Vital Statistics, Statehouse
Boise 83720

ILLINOIS $3.00
State Department of Public Health
Springfield 62761

INDIANA $3.00
State Board of Health
Indianapolis 46206

IOWA $2.00
State Department of Health
Des Moines 50319

KANSAS $3.00
Bureau of Registration and Health Statistics
Topeka 66620

KENTUCKY $4.00
Department of Human Resources, Vital Statistics
275 Main Street
Frankfort 40621

LOUISIANA $2.00
Office of Vital Records, P.O. Box 60630
New Orleans 70160

MAINE $2.00
State Department of Health and Welfare
Augusta 04333

MARYLAND $2.00
State Department of Health and Mental Hygiene
Baltimore 21203

MASSACHUSETTS $2.00
Registrar of Vital Statistics
Boston 02108

MICHIGAN $3.00
Office of Vital and Health Statistics
Lansing 48914

MINNESOTA $3.00
State Department of Health
Minneapolis 55440

MISSISSIPPI $6.00
State Board of Health
Jackson 39205

MISSOURI $1.00
State Department of Public Health and Welfare
Jefferson City 65101

MONTANA $2.00
State Department of Health
Helena 59601

NEBRASKA $3.00
Department of Human Resources
Carson 89710

NEW HAMPSHIRE $3.00
Bureau of Vital Statistics, 61 S. Spring Street
Concord 03301

NEW JERSEY $2.50
State Department of Health
Trenton 08625

NEW MEXICO $2.00
New Mexico Health and Social Services Department
Santa Fe 87503

NEW YORK $2.00
State Department of Health
Albany

NEW YORK CITY $3.50
Department of Health of New York City
New York City 10013

NORTH CAROLINA $3.00
State Board of Health
P.0. Box 2091, Raleigh 27602

NORTH DAKOTA $2.00
Divison of Vital Records
Bismark 58505

OHIO $2.00
State Department of Health
Columbus 43215

OKLAHOMA $2.00
State Department of Health, P.O. Box 53551
Oklahoma City 73105

OREGON $5.00
State Board of Health
Portland 97207

PENNSYLVANIA $4.00
State Department of Health
New Castle 16103

RHODE ISLAND $2.00
State Department of Health
Providence 02909

SOUTH CAROLINA $3.00
State Department of Health
Columbus 29203

SOUTH DAKOTA $2.00
State Department of Health
Pierre 57501

TENNESSEE $3.00
State Department of Public Health
Nashville 37219

TEXAS $3.00
State Department of Health
Austin 78701

UTAH $3.50
Utah State Department of Health
Salt Lake City 84110

VERMONT Public Health Statistics Division, Dept. of Health Burlington 05401	$2.00
VIRGINIA Department of Health Richmond 23208	$3.00
VIRGIN ISLANDS St. Thomas Registrar of Vital Statistics St. Thomas 00802	$2.00
WASHINGTON Vital Records, P.O. Box 9709 Olympia 98504	$3.00
WEST VIRGINIA State Department of Health Charleston 25305	$2.00
WISCONSIN Wisconsin Division of Health Madison 53701	$4.00
WYOMING Wyoming Division of Health and Medical Services Cheyenne 82002	$2.00

Fictitious Business Name Filing

These little gems are generally county filed documents issued at the county courthouse. The Fictitious Business Filing is the legal permission necessary for the applicant to conduct a busines in a name other than their own. Earlier I stated you should use:

Your Name, Researcher

as a business title. By doing so, you should have avoided the requirement of filing a Fictitious Business Name Statement and the cost of doing so. If your subject is in business and is using any name other than their own they must file a fictitious business statement. If they have not, chances are they are not in business or their business does not involve the use of money. Without such a statement, a bank will not open an account in any name but your legal birth name. I do know cases, however, where a subject used a very large cash deposit instead of a fictitious name statement to open a business account. Most "small fish," however, do not have such means and play by the rules.

On page 46, is an example of a typical fictitious name statement form. If your subject has ever filed such a document, you will undoubtedly thank the clerk; government employees rarely leave a blank unfilled. A document such as this could crack your case wide open.

County Licenses and Permits

Like cities many counties regulate activities within their boundaries. If your target county does, index your subject's name against the county files. Check with the county police for accident reports and traffic violations also.

Welfare and Unemployment

These records are confidential and are not available to the public. Without "inside sources" (employees who have access to their files), you will positively obtain no information from them.

NOT VALID UNLESS CLERK'S ENDORSEMENT APPEARS BELOW

REMINDER
1. Submit original and 3 copies.
2. Filing fee $10.00 for one business name,
   $2.00 for each additional business name;
   $2.00 for each additional partner after first two.
3. Provide return envelope, if mailed.

SEE REVERSE SIDE FOR INSTRUCTIONS

FICTITIOUS BUSINESS NAME STATEMENT

THE FOLLOWING PERSON(S) IS(ARE) DOING BUSINESS AS: (TYPE ALL INFORMATION)

1.	Fictitious Business Name(s)
2.	Street Address, City & State of Principal place of Business in California Zip Code

3.

Full name of Registrant   (if corporation - show state of incorporation)

Residence Address	City	State	Zip Code

Full name of Registrant   (if corporation show state of incorporation)

Residence Address	City	State	Zip Code

Full name of Registrant   (if corporation show state of incorporation)

Residence Address	City	State	Zip Code

Full name of Registrant   (if corporation - show state of incorporation)

Residence Address	City	State	Zip Code

4. This business is conducted by ( ) an individual ( ) a general partnership ( ) a limited partnership
( ) an unincorporated association other than a partnership ( ) a corporation ( ) a business trust   (CHECK ONE ONLY)

5.

If Registrant a corporation sign below:

Corporation Name _____

Signed _____

Signature & Title _____

Typed or Printed _____

_____
(TYPED OR PRINTED)

This statement was filed with the County Clerk of Orange County on date indicated by file stamp above.

CERTIFICATION
I hereby certify that the foregoing is a correct copy of the original on file in my office.
Lee A. Branch, County Clerk

By _____Deputy

FILE NO._____

F0182-266.6 (R 1/82)

FILE WITH COUNTY CLERK

LOS ANGELES COUNTY CLERK

INFORMATION FOR ALL INDIVIDUALS AND FIRMS OPERATING UNDER FICTITIOUS NAMES

REQUIREMENT FOR FILING FICTITIOUS BUSINESS NAME STATEMENT

Chapter 5 (commencing with Section 17900) of Part 3 of Division 7 of the Business and Professions Code, requires the filing of a Fictitious Business Name Statement.

WHO MUST FILE

Every individual, partnership and other associations and corporations who regularly transact business for profit in this state under a fictitious business name.

DEFINITIONS OF A FICTITIOUS FIRM NAME

FOR INDIVIDUALS: A name that does not include the surname of the individual. A name that suggests existence of additional owners (such words as "Company," "& Company," "& Associates," "Brothers," but not words to merely describe the business being conducted).

FOR PARTNERSHIPS or other associations of persons: A name that does not include surname of each general partner or a name that suggests existence of additional owners (such as "Company," "Brothers," etc.). (In the case of an unincorporated association other than a partnership, a "general partner" means a person whose liability in the business is substantially the same as a general partner.)

FOR CORPORATIONS: A name not stated in its articles of incorporation.

ORGANIZATIONS NOT INCLUDED: Non-profit corporations or associations such as churches, labor unions, fraternal and charitable organizations, non-profit hospitals, etc., and, real estate investment trusts with permits under Section 23002 Government Code which have statements on file designating agent for service of process.

WHEN TO FILE

The statement must be filed not later than 40 days from the time business commences to be transacted.

WHERE TO FILE

The fictitious business name statement shall be filed with the County Clerk of the county in which the registrant has his principal place of business. If he has no place of business in California, it shall be filed with the County Clerk of Sacramento County.

PUBLICATION

Within thirty days after the statement is filed, the registrant will publish it in a newspaper of general circulation in the county in which the principal place of business is located. "The newspaper selected for the publication of the statement should be one that circulates in the area where the business is to be conducted." (Section 17917b, Business & Professions Code).

If the county has no newspaper of general circulation, it will be published in an adjoining county. If the registrant does not have a place of business in the state, publication will be made in Sacramento County.

An affidavit of publication shall be filed with the County Clerk within 30 days after the completion of publication.

EXPIRATIONS

A fictitious business name statement expires at the end of five years from December 31 of the year it was filed with the County Clerk, and a new statement must be filed. The new statement need not be re-published if there has been no change in the information contained in the statement previously filed.

A statement expires 40 days after any change in the facts contained in the statement except that a change in the residence address of an individual does not cause it to expire.

A statement expires when an abandonment has been filed.

ABANDONMENTS

A person who has filed a statement may, upon ceasing to transact business in this state under that fictitious name, file a statement of abandonment, publish same and file an affidavit of publication. Forms for this purpose are available in the County Clerk's Office.

WITHDRAWAL OF A GENERAL PARTNER

A general partner of a partnership having a statement on file may file a statement of withdrawal, publish and file an affidavit of publication. (Publication is not required if dissolution of the partnership has been published pursuant to the Corporations Code.) Forms for this purpose are available in the County Clerk's Office.

TRUSTEES, GUARDIANS, ADMINISTRATORS, ASSIGNEES AND PURCHASERS

Whenever failure to comply with this law would preclude taking legal action to recover monies due, a trustee in bankruptcy, an administrator of the estate, an assignee or purchaser of the business may file the fictitious name statement.

FEES

The fee for filing a fictitious business name statement is $10, which includes one certified copy of the statement.

The fee for filing a statement of abandonment is $2.

The fee for filing a statement of withdrawal from partnership is $5.

The Certified Copies of any statement on file will be furnished for a fee of $2.

QUESTIONS AND ANSWERS

QUESTION: What information is contained in divorce records?

ANSWER: Divorces are Superior-Civil proceedings and fall into two basic catagories: Uncontested and Contested. Uncontested are typically "friendly" divorces in which both parties have reached a settlement prior to their coming into court. The court is simply the vehicle to make the separation and settlement legal. On the other hand, a Contested Divorce is usually more hostile and typically centers around child custody or property ownership issues.

In either case, divorce records are public and contain a wealth of information. Names, (both parties) full and maiden, Social Security numbers, addresses, children's names, real property listings, tax records, business information (should either party own one), automobiles, furnishings, names of relatives in many cases, names of friends and witnesses, names of employer, full credit and debt information and more can be found in the case files.

Usually divorce records are indexed right along with the Superior Court filings and may be coded by a "D" preceeding the case number. Ask the court clerk for help.

QUESTION: I know businesses go to court also. Where do I look for court filings on businesses my subject may have owned?

ANSWER: Business filings make up the bulk of civil filings. They are filed in the same indexes as one would find an individual. Much like other proceedings those involving businesses are very detailed. Most cases involving a business last for years. The files can be huge. The average file would probably be larger than this book.

So if you know your subject owned a business, be sure to index the business name as well as your subject.

QUESTION: What if my subject declared bankruptcy and now cannot be found? What court do I check then?

ANSWER: Federal Bankruptcy Court; we will discuss this in Section 4.6.

4.4 STATE RECORD AND FILES

Department of Motor Vehicles:

The Department of Motor Vehicles' records are available to the public. The records can be indexed in several ways, but essentially all that is required is a complete name, driver's license number, or a vehicle license plate number. Anyone of these individually will enable you to obtain the other two.

Additionally available are complete driving and accident histories, mailing and residential addresses and of course full descriptions of any vehicles registered to any one individual or entity. Some states also provide a full description of the driver including age, Social Security number, and even a picture!

For heavy users of such information, most states provide open accounts and data base accessibility. The information is then available over the phone at anytime and the user is billed once a month. For infrequent use, I suggest you contact your local DMV, and ask how the information can best be obtained. Test the procedure by checking your own name, and examine the results.

If accidents are reported, you may have to go to the reporting authority to obtain copies of the report. On page 50, I have provided you with a standard request form. Call the station first, and get the application details. Then mail in the request and required fee, if any. The police are responsive to these types of requests and will be more than happy to handle it for you.

The following is a list of the departments you can write to in order to obtain driving history transcripts. Arkansas, North Carolina, Pennsylvania, Wisconsin and Washington are the only states that are problems. Be sure to send the required fee. Call first to ensure you use the proper procedure.

APPLICATION FOR RELEASE OF REPORT OR PHOTOGRAPHS

FILE NO: _____

DATE OCCURRED: _____ LOCATION: _____

KIND OF REQUEST: TRAFFIC ACCIDENT: _____ PHOTOS: _____

CRIME INCIDENT REPORT: _____ Specify Crime/Indicent _____

NAME OF DRIVER (Traffic Accident) VICTIM (Crime/Indicent): _____

_____

PERSONS INVOLVED, IMMEDIATE FAMILY MEMBERS OR GUARDIAN, ATTORNEY OR AUTHORIZED INDIVIDUAL REPRESENTING INVOLVED PERSON, REPRESENTATIVES OF INSURANCE COMPANIES, VICTIMS OF CRIME, COMLETE SECTIONS BELOW:

This will certify that I am, or I represent _____
who was:

__ DRIVER __ PASSENGER __ PEDESTRIAN __ PROPERTY OWNER INVOLVED

__ VICTIM OF CRIME/INCIDENT - and that I have a proper interest in this

accident as __ WIFE __ HUSBAND __ MOTHER __ FATHER __ DAUGHTER __ SON

__ GUARDIAN __ AGENT __ VICTIM ____ OTHER (explain below)

PRINT NAME _____ PHONE # _____

SIGNATURE _____ DATE _____

ADDRESS _____ CITY _____

ZIP _____

_____

TOTAL FEE $ _____ RECEIPT # _____ REC'D BY _____

PPD 5 (Rev. 11-6-79)

States with which we can run driving record with just name and DDL# or name & date of birth:

Alaska	New Jersey
Arizona	New Mexico
Colorado	North Carolina
Connecticut	North Dakota
Delaware	Ohio
District of Columbia	Oklahoma
Florida	Oregon
Indiana SS# is DDL#	Rhode Island
Kentucky	South Carolina
Louisiana	South Dakota
Maine	Tennessee
Maryland	Texas
Michigan	Utah
Minnisota	Vermont
Mississippi SS# is DDL#	Virginia
Montana	West Virginia
Nebraska	Wisconsin
Nevada	Wyoming
New Hampshire	

States which need the person's written permission:

Arkansas	Kansas
Georgia (no alpha files)	Pennsylvania
Hawaii SS# is DDL#	

States which need the drivers license number:

Alabama	Iowa SS# is DDL#
Idaho	Missouri
Illinois	

New York needs name & New York drivers license number or name, date of birth and last known address in New York.

Massachusetts and Washington are the only two states in which we can not run a drivers license check.

FOR DRIVING HISTORY TRANSCRIPTS WRITE:

ALABAMA ($2.00)
Drivers License Division
Certificate Section
P.O. Box 1471
Montgomery 36102

ALASKA ($2.00)
Department of Public Safety
Drivers License Safety
Pouch N
Juneau 99801

ARIZONA ($2.00)
Motor Vehicle Division
1801 West Jefferson Street
Phoenix 85007

ARKANSAS
Office of Drivers Services
Traffic Violation Report Unit
P.O. Box 1272
Little Rock 72203

CALIFORNIA ($6.00)
Department of Motor Vehicles
P.O. Box 11231
Sacramento 95813

COLORADO ($5.00)
Department of Revenue
Motor Vehicle Division
Master File Section
140 West 6th Avenue
Denver 80204

NOTE: I've left space to pen in new addresses should find any of these have changed.

CONNECTICUT ($4.00)
Department of Motor Vehicles
Copy Record Section
60 State Street
Wethersfield 06109

DELAWARE ($2.00)
Department of Motor Vehicles
P.0. Box 698
Dover 19901

DISTRICT OF COLUMBIA
Dept. of Transportation
Bureau of Motor Vehicles
301 C. Street N.W..
Washington

FLORIDA ($3.00)
Drivers License Division
Department of Highway Safety
Kirkham Building
Tallahassee 32301

GEORGIA ($2.00)
Department of Public Safety
Drivers Service Section
P.0. Box 1456
Atlanta 30301

HAWAII ($3.00)
Dist. of the lst Circuit
Violations Bureau
824 Bethel
Honolulu 96813

IDAHO ($5.00)
Dept. of Law Enforcement
Motor Vehicle Division
P.0. Box 34
Boise 83731

ILLINOIS ($5.00)
Sec. of State
Drivers Services Section
2701 South Dirksen Parkway
Springfield 62723

INDIANA ($1.00)
Bureau of Motor Vehicles
Pall Mall Section
Room 416 State Office Building
Indianapolis 46204

IOWA ($1.00)
Dept. of Transportation
Records Section
Lacas Building
Des Moines 50319

KANSAS ($3.00)
Division of Vehicles
Driver Control Bureau
State Office Building
Topeka 66626

KENTUCKY: ($2.00)
Division of Driver Licenses
New State Office Building
Frankfort 40601

LOUISIANA ($2.00)
Department of Public Safety
Drivers License Division
O.D.R. Section, Box 1271
Baton Rouge 70821

MAINE ($3.00)
Sec. of State
Motor Vehicle Division
1 Child Street
Augusta 04333

MASSACHUSETTS
Registry of Motor Vehicles
Court Records Section
100 Nashua Street
Boston 02114

MICHIGAN ($3.00)
Dept. of State Bureau of Drivers Services
Commercial Look-up Unit
7064 Crowner Drive
Lansing 49818

MINNESOTA ($2.00)
Department of Public Safety
Drivers license Office
Room 108 State Highway Building
St. Paul 55155

MISSISSIPPI ($3.00)
Mississippi Highway Safety Patrol
Drivers License Insurance Bureau
P.O. Box 958
Jackson 39205

MISSOURI ($1.00)
Bureau of Driver Licenses
P.O. Box 200
Department of Revenue
Jefferson City 65101

MONTANA ($2.00)
Montana Highway Patrol
303 Roberts
Helena 59601

NEBRASKA ($.75)
Department of Motor Vehicles
Driver Records Section
P.O. Box 94789
Lincoln 68509

NEW HAMPSHIRE ($5.00)
Division of Motor Vehicles
Driver Record Research Unit
85 Loudon Road
Concord 03301

NEW JERSEY ($5.00)
Division of Motor Vehicles
Bureau of Security Responsibility
25 S. Montgomery Street
Trenton

NEW MEXICO
Transportation Department
Driver Services Bureau
Manual Lajan Sr. Building
Santa Fe 87503

NEW YORK ($2.00)
Department of Motor Vehicles
Public Services Department
Empire State Plaza
Albany 12228

NORTH CAROLINA ($1.00)
Traffic Records Section
Division of Motor Vehicles
Raleigh

NORTH DAKOTA ($2.00)
Drivers License Division
Capitol Grounds
Bismark 58505

OHIO ($5.00)
Bureau of Motor Vehicles
P.O. Box 16520
Columbus 43216

OKLAHOMA ($3.00)
Driver Records Service
Department of Public Safety
P.O. Box 11415
Oklahoma City 73136

OREGON ($6.00)
Motor Vehicle Division
1905 Lona Avenue
Salem 97314

PENNSYLVANIA ($1.50)
Department of Transportation
Bureau of Accident Analysis
Operation Information Section
Room 212, Transportation and Safety Building
Harrisburg 17120

RHODE ISLAND ($1.50)
Registry of Motor Vehicles
Room 101 G, State Office Building
Providence 02903

SOUTH CAROLINA ($3.00)
Department of Highways and Public Transportation
Drivers Records Clerk, Section 201
Columbia 29216

SOUTH DAKOTA ($2.00)
Department of Public Safety
Driver Improvement Program
118 West Capital
Pierce 57501

TENNESSEE ($3.00)
Department of Public Safety
Jackson Building
Nashville 37219

TEXAS ($4.00)
Department of Public Safety
License Issuance and Driver Records
P.O. Box 4087
Austin 78773

UTAH ($1.00)
Drivers License Division
314 State Office Building
Salt Lake City 84114

VERMONT ($3.00)
Agency Transportation
Department of Motor Vehicles
Montpelier 05602

VIRGINIA
Division of Motor Vehicles
Driver Licensing and Information
P.O. Box 27412
Richmond 23269

WASHINGTON ($1.50)
Division of Licensing
Department of Motor Vehicles
Olympia 98501

WEST VIRGINIA ($1.00)
Driver Improvement Division
Department of Motor Vehicles
1800 Washington Street
Charleston 25305

WISCONSIN ($4.00)
Department of Transportation
Driver Record File
P.O. Box 7918
Madison 53707

WYOMING ($2.00)
Department of Revenue
2200 Carey Avenue
Cheyenne 82001

In order to trace a license plate, title or registration, write or call the appropriate state office. Many states provide license plate traces and title information over the phone. Local and state police also have this capability. Running a plate typically reveals the name of the registered owner, the legal owner (usually a bank or a credit union) and the registerd owner's address.

For Title, Registration or Tag Information, Write:

ALABAMA: (205) 832-6740
Will send bill.
State of Alabama
P.O. Box 104
Motor Vehicle and License Division
Department of Revenue
Montgomery 36130

ALASKA: (906) 349-4581
State of Alaska
Department of Motor Vehicles
P.O. Box 960
Anchorage 99510

ARIZONA: (602) 261-7011
State of Arizona
Department of Transportation
Motor Vehicles - Complete Record Division
1801 W. Jefferson Avenue
Phoenix 85007

CALIFORNIA: (916) 322-2498
State of California
Department of Motor Vehicles
P.O. Box 2747
Sacramento 95812

NOTE: Again I've left space to pen in new addresses should find any of these have changed.

COLORADO: (303) 839-3422
State of Colorado
Department of Revenue
Motor Vehicle Division
Master File
140 West Sixth Avenue
Denver 80204

CONNECTICUT: (203) 566-2640
State of Connecticut
Department of Motor Vehicles
60 State Street
Wethersfield 06109

DELAWARE: (302) 678-4462
State of Delaware Motor Vehicle Director
Motor Vehicle Division
State Highway Administration Building
P.O. Box 698
Dover 19901

DISTRICT OF COLUMBIA: (202) 727-6680
District of Columbia
Department of Motor Vehicles, Registrar
301 C. Street N.W. 20001

FLORIDA: (904) 488-5056
State of Florida
Department of Highway Safety
Division of Motor Vehicles
Correspondence Section
Tallahassee

GEORGIA: (404) 656-4100
State of Georgia
Motor Vehicle Unit
Department of Revenue
Atlanta

HAWAII: (808) 955-8221
Address Unknown
(Each island has different departments)
State of Hawaii

ILLINOIS: (217) 782-1059
State of Illinois
Secretary of State
Sixth Floor
Centennial Building
Springfield 62756

INDIANA (317) 633-4119
State of Indiana
Bureau of Motor Vehicles
314 State Office Building
Pall Mall Department
Indianapolis 46204

IOWA: (515) 281-5817
State of Iowa
Department of Transportation
Office of Vehicle Registration
Lucas State Office Building
Des Moines 50319

KANSAS: (913) 296-3621
State of Kansas
Department of Revenue
Division of Motor Vehicles
Attention: Verification
Topeka 66626

KENTUCKY: (502) 564-8000
Kentucky State Police
Department, Auto Theft Unit
New State Office Building, Room 111
Frankfort 40601

LOUISIANA: (504) 925-6353
State of Louisiana
Department of Public Safety
Vehicle Registration Bureau
P.O. Box 66196
Baton Rouge 70896

MAINE: (207) 207-3556
State of Maine
Secretary of State
Motor Vehicle Department
Augusta 04333

MARYLAND: (301) 577-5600
State of Maryland
Motor Vehicle Administration
6601 Richie Highway, N.E.
Glen Burie 21061

MASSACHUSETTS: (617) 727-3794
Commonwealth of Massachusetts
Service Unit B
Reg. of Motor Vehicles (Drivers License)
100 Nashua Street
Boston 02114

MICHIGAN: (517) 322-1624
State of Michigan
Department of Public Safety
Driver and Vehicle Services
Lansing 48918

MINNESOTA: (612) 296-7931
State of Minnesota
Department of Public Safety
Driver and Vehicle Services Division
Transportation Building, Room 108
St. Paul 55155

MISSISSIPPI: (601) 354-6407
State of Mississippi
Department of Motor Vehicles Comptroller
Title Division
P.O. Box 1383
Jackson 39205

MISSOURI: (314) 751-4509
State of Missouri
Departent of Revenue
Motor Vehicle Bureau
P.O. Box 100
Jefferson City 65701

MONTANA: (406) 846-1423
State of Montana
Registrar's Bureau
925 Main Street, Deer Lodge 58722
State of Montana Highway Patrol
Scott Hart Building
Driver License Records, Helena

NEBRASKA: (402) 471-2281
State of Nebraska
Department of Motor Vehicles
301 Centennial Mall
Lincoln 68509
Driver Record Office
P.O. Box 94789
Lincoln 68509

NEVADA: (702) 855-5505
Nevada Research, Inc.
555 Wrightway
Carson City 89711
206 North Curry
Carson City 89701

NEW HAMPSHIRE: (603) 271-3111
State of New Hampshire
Department of Public Safety
Division of Motor Vehicles
John O. Morton Building
Concord 03301

NEW JERSEY: (609) 292-4102
State of New Jersey
Division of Motor Vehicles
Certified Information
25 South Montgomery Street
Trenton 08666

NEW MEXICO: (505) 827-2173
State of New Mexico
Department of Motor Vehicles
Title and Registration
Manual Lujan Sr. Building
Santa Fe 87503

NEW YORK: (508) 474-0791
State of New York
Department of Motor Vehicles
Rockefeller Plaza
Albany 12228
Attention: Title Bureau/or Registrations

NORTH CAROLINA: (919) 733-4241
State of North Carolina
Department of Motor Vehicles (Registration Division)
(Driver's License Division)
1100 New Bern Avenue
Raleigh 27697

NORTH DAKOTA (701) 224-2724
State of North Dakota
Department of Motor Vehicles
State Office Building
9th and Boulevard
Records Department
Bismark 58505

OHIO: (614) 466-3300
State of Ohio
Department of Highway Safety
Bureau of Motor Vehicles
4300 Kimberly Parkway
Columbus 43227

OKLAHOMA: (405) 521-3221
State of Oklahoma
Tax Commission
Motor Vehicle Divison
2501 Lincoln Blvd.
Oklahoma City 73194

OREGON: (503) 378-6935
State of Oregon
Motor Vehicle Division
1905 Lana Avenue, N.E.
Salem 97310

PENNSYLVANIA: (717) 787-3130
State of Pennsylvania
Bureau of Motor Vehicles
Paid Information Department, Room 210A
Harrisburg 17122

RHODE ISLAND: (803) 758-3461
State of South Carolina
Motor Vehicle Division, State Highway Department
Columbia 29216

SOUTH CAROLINA: (803) 758-3461
State of South Carolina
Motor Vehicle Division, State Highway Department
Columbia 29216

SOUTH DAKOTA: (605) 773-3541
State of South Dakota
Department of Public Safety
118 West Capitol Avenue
Pierre 57501

TENNESSEE: (615) 741-2477
State of Tennessee
Department of Revenue
Title and Records Section
Motor Vehicle Division
Andrew Jackson Building
Nashville 37424

TEXAS: (512) 475-7611
State of Texas
Motor Vehicle Divison
Department of Highway and Public Transportation
40th and Jackson Avenue
Austin 78779

UTAH: (801) 533-5311
State of Utah
State Tax Commission
Motor Vehicle Division
State Fair Grounds
1905 Motor Avenue
Salt Lake City 84416

VERMONT: (802) 828-2121
State of Venmont
Department of Motor Vehicles
Driver's License Division
State Street
Montpelier 05603

VIRGINIA: (804) 257-0523
Commonwealth of Virginia
Department of Motor Vehicles
P.O. Box 27412
Richmond 23269

WASHINGTON: (206) 753-6990
State of Washington
Driver's Licensing
P.O. Box 9909
Olympia 98504

WEST VIRGINIA: (304) 348-3900
State of West Virginia
Department of Motor Vehicles
1800 Washington Street, East
Charleston 25303

WISCONSIN: (608) 266-1321

WYOMING:
Department of Revenue and Taxation
Motor Vehicle Division
2200 Carey Avenue
Cheyenne 82002

In many states the driver's license number is coded. In California it indicates the year issued as demonstrated in the list below.

Permanent California Driver's License and ID Card Number Series

Date First Issued	Starting Number	Ending Number
1-2-44	V0001001	V0776882
1-2-45	W0001001	W1082899
1-2-46	Y0001001	Y1331399
1-2-47	Z0001001	Z1087399
1-2-48	B0001001	B2086799
1-2-52	D0001001	D0999999
2-2-54	F0001001	F0999999
4-4-56	G0001001	G0762480
9-11-57	H0001001	H0999999
1-12-59	J0001001	J0999999
9-13-60	K0001001	K0630587
9-15-61	M0001001	M0999999
5-7-63	K0630588	K0999999
11-22-63	P0001001	P0999999
5-20-65	R0001001	R0999999
11-15-66	S0001001	S0999999
5-23-68	A0001001	A0999999
9-25-69	E0001001	E0999999
12-14-70	N0001001	N0999999
3-30-72	N2001001	N2700464
1-2-73	N3001001	N3851691
1-2-74	N4001001	N4849500
1-2-75	N5001001	N5887700
1-2-76	N6001001	N6978900
1-3-77	N7001001	N7999999
12-2-77	N7001001	V7087050
1-5-78	N8001001	N8999999
11-29-78	V8001001	V8151600
1-25-79	N9001001	N9999999
12-31-79	V9001001	V9451001
1-1-80	C0001001	C0999999
11-15-80	U0001001	U0999999
1-15-81	C1001001	C1999999
11-4-81	U1001001	U1211500
1-15-82	C2001001	C3000000
1-15-83	C4000000	C5000000
1-15-84	C5000000	C6000000
1-15-85	C6000000	C7000000

I know other states do this as well. Should you obtain your subject's drivers license number, write or call the appropriate regulating authority and ask. The information may be helpful. Also find out if they can tell you where (city or county) the license was obtained. Knowing it would be a perfect place to start your search.

Another interesting source of information is the National Driver Registration Service. This service was established several years ago to help law enforcement and insurance companies keep track of drivers with suspended or revoked licenses in one state, who reapply in another. For more details write:

> National Driver Registration Service
> U.S. Department of Commerce
> 1717 H Street
> Washington D.C.

State Board of Corporations

We have talked some about businesses and their importance in locating missing persons. The corporation is usually thought of as a very large business. This is not true. Any business regardless of size can be a corporation. Even an individual can be a corporation but usually a corporation is some type of business.

Businesses can be:

1. sole proprietorships
2. a partnership
3. a corporation

By making a business a corporation the business is entitled to certain rights not afforded to the other types of businesses. The most important one I suppose, is the legal protection it gives its owners (now called directors). By law, they are not responsible for corporate debt or liability, unless personal guarantees have been given. In other words, should the business go bankrupt, the directors are not held personally responsible for its debts and will not lose their personal property as a result. Not a bad deal, huh? This, however, is not a "free lunch". Operating a corporation is a precise and heavily regulated matter. In fact, all states control the conduct of corporations within their boundaries. To our delight, these records are public.

Corporation filings contain the name of the corporation, its business address, business mailing address, names of all of the directors, President, Vice-President, Treasurer, and Secretary, their resident addresses and telephone numbers (sometimes), date filed, and type of business, product and/or service.

If the corporation is public (stock traded in a recognized public market) substantial stock holders are also listed. Additionally, the corporation must be registered with the

Securities Exchange Commission, (the SEC) where intimate financial details of the Company's officers, major stock holders, and of the business itself are exposed. Additionally, the corporation must produce and make public an annual report detailing every aspect, good and bad, about the company, its operations and officers. Most states provide corporation information over the phone. However, complete filing details must always be written for. For more information write the appropriate State Board of Corporations.

State Franchise Tax Board

More commonly known as the State Tax Board, this agency is responsible for administering and collecting state income tax. In many states tax information on businesses is public information. But in no state is State Income Tax on an individual public. Write or call your state today for more details.

State Board of Equalization

These nifty bureaucrats are responsible for administering and collecting state sales tax. Any business involved in the sale of a product on a retail level in a state having sales tax, must file. Services are generally not taxed. Typically, the application for filing is available to the public. If available, it should contain the applicant's name, business name, resident address, business address, phone numbers, bank and account numbers (so the state can locate assets if necessary), type of business and estimated annual gross sales.

Some states also have similar filings for businesses which operate on a wholesale level. Wholesalers usually are not taxed for sales tax purposes, but states generally like to keep track of who's selling what.

State Licensing Board

All states regulate trades and professions within their boundaries. One would be surprised to know how much is licensed and regulated. Should you suspect your subject has a trade or profession which may be regulated, contact the State Board of Licensing.

California probably regulates and licenses more professionals than any other state. Here is a partial list:

Aircraft Mechanics	Doctors
Airports	Electricians
Alarm Installers	Engineers
Alcohol Sales	Explosives
Auctioneers	Explosive Storage
Auto Inspectors	Fishing and Hunting
Auto Wreckers	Food Processing
Bankers	Fuel Storage
Barbers	Fuel Transportation
Bill Collectors	Furniture Manufacturing
Builders/Carpenters	Gambling
Building Contractors	Garment Cleaners
Building Wreckers	Insurance
Carpet Cleaners	Investigators
Certified Public Accountants	Labs
Child Care/Daycare	Lawyers
Dentists	Marriage Counseling
Mattress Rebuilders	Plumbers
Meat Packers	Police
Meat Storage	Polluters
Mechanics	Process Servers
Mining	Public Transportation
Movie Theaters	Real Estate Agents and Brokers
Notary Public	Restaurants
Nursing Homes	Scrap Dealers
Nurses	Security Guards
Oil Drilling	Service Stations
Painters	Stock Brokers
Pawnbrokers	Surveyors
Pet Groomers	Taxis
Pest Controllers	Teachers
Pharmacists	Therapists
Pilots	Timbering
Public Utilities	Trade Schools
Veterinarians	Water Taxis
Waste Disposal	Waste Storage
Waste Removal	Weights & Measures
X-Ray Technicians	Zoos

If your subject owns a business involving one of these or is himself a professional, chances are they are licensed. Records concerning licenses and applications for licenses are public.

States are very good in keeping their information up to date. If not, how could they collect those annual licensing fees? This information is always available by phone. Use your phone book or call information. Call the appropriate office and ask for a license search in the name of your subject. If they are licensed, you will be provided with an updated address, phone number and full assortment of other useful details.

Vessels And Aircraft

Many states require registration of vessels and aircraft with their departments of Motor Vehicles. Others have established individual agencies for these special forms of transportation. However regulated or documented, these records are also public.

Be sure to check under your subject's name and business name if applicable.

Workmens' Compensation Board

Today all legal employees (and in some states such as California, illegal employees and aliens) are covered under some form of workmens' compensation insurance. This state regulated insurance program provides the employees an assortment of benefits and compensations in the event they are injured while on the job.

These records are public and yours for the asking. They are generally accessed on a county level and often contain what would be otherwise concidered confidential medical information. Call first and get the details.

State Police

State Police perform a number of different functions, but one of their most important is Highway Patrol. As a result, they respond and investigate traffic accidents on state highways. Consequently accident reports are made and filed. In most states they are yours just for the asking, along with a small fee (generally around $5.00). Some states only provide them to those directly involved or their insurance company. In those cases, you must become the "victim," never a witness (police are always looking for witnesses) or an "insurance representative." In either case, employ a pretext that is appropriate with your known information and ask for the report. Keep in mind you will be calling a clerk, not a police officer.

Use of a pre-typed form is the best; see mine from the California Highway Patrol. A completed form and a business card will get you your needed information. Sometimes, you may be able to get crime and arrest reports in a similar fashion. If in doubt, call first. If you need the information from an out-of-state source, call first then write.

Chances are any report obtained will contain confidential information and that is what you are looking for. Current addresses, current and sometimes unlisted phone numbers, next of kin, current employer, current work phone, names of other people in the subject's car, etc. Also contained will be vehicle information. When in doubt, check it out.

I once found a woman a major insurance company had sought for years, simply by obtaining a traffic accident report. The report of course contained a ficticious resident address but the phone number was good. Within minutes of receiving the report she unwittingly gave me her address. The entire process cost me several dollars and two long distance phone calls. My client was so pleased he showered me with hours of additional and very profitable work for weeks.

4.5 FEDERAL

Federal Court

Like state municipal and superior court systems, Federal courts can be indexed and their files examined. If they are readily accessible to you, I recommend you search them. If not I will show you where you can find the same information.

Incidentally, Federal courts rule over all Federal law, and any interstate issues. The United States Supreme Court is the highest Federal Court.

Bankruptcy Court

Bankruptcy is a federal issue, and is decided in Federal Court. Bankruptcy and **reorganization** under Bankruptcy is normally filed under a chapter (seven, eleven or thirteen) of the Federal Bankruptcy Code. A judge is then appointed to preside and rule over the hearing and make all final decisions.

Regardless of the circumstances, all records are public. In the case of a personal bankruptcy, every detail of one's finances and personal life are spelled out for the court (and you).

Many people in financial difficulty seek protection under bankruptcy as the procedure is so easy and ramifications so slight. If your subject ever declared bankruptcy, the Federal Court should be your next stop. When indexing, be sure to index spouses and businesses. I have found people by finding their friends in bankruptcy court; you might also.

There are three types of bankruptcies you need to know about.

    I. CHAPTER VII - Also known as a standard bankruptcy for business.

        A. This chapter is for debtors without non-exempt assets (typically a business).

        B. Debtors may refile every 7 years.

    II. CHAPTER XI - The reorganization plan for debtors who own a business or are self-employed professionals. Also known as reorganization.

        A. This chapter is for a debtor that overextended themselves, but feels that given enough time and expert help they can reorganize their debt to income ratio and pay their bills.

B. Unsecured Creditors, particularly the largest 15, are invited by the bankruptcy judge to serve on the Creditor's Committee to oversee the debtor's reorganization. This Committee is very powerful in determining that the debt repayment actually complies with the laws and regulations in an accurate, businesslike and timely manner. The Committee even has the right to replace the debtor as head of his own business in order to preserve the assets of the bankrupt estate.

C. This bankruptcy chapter is usually converted to a Chapter VII bankruptcy, when the debtor fails at their efforts to reorganize.

D. The debtor under Chapter XI must propose a repayment schedule to the bankruptcy court for approval within a specific period of time. Many businesses operate in Chapter XI for years!

III. CHAPTER XIII - The adjustment of debts of an individual with regular income.

A. The debts of the debtor are paid according to a payment plan, which must not exceed a 36-month period of time.

B. This plan often pays a percentage of the debt rather than in full.

C. The debtor may refile immediately after completion of one plan (and often due).

The Federal Communications Commission

The F.C.C. licenses every form of communication including telephones and computer interface systems. These records and applications are also public. Call or write your nearest office for details.

Federal Aviation Administration

The F.A.A. regulates and licenses all aspects of aviation including balloons and gliders. If appropriate, check with them. Their records are public.

Federal Aviation Administration
Aeronautics Center
P.O. Box 25082
Oklahoma City, OK 73125

Internal Revenue Service

As a matter of practice, the I.R.S. will provide "the date of last return" on anyone or any business, which includes the address to which the return was sent. All you need to provide is the full name and Social Security Number. For businesses a Federal Tax Number is required. For details, contact the nearest Regional Office. I suggest you make the request first, then ask for the procedures. That way, while you are waiting for their procedure, they are in the possession of and working on your original request.

Interstate Commerce Commission

This group of individuals regulate and license all forms of interstate commercial transportation. If your subject is a trucker, or in the trucking or transportation business, you will find them in these records. All records are public and phone searches are accepted.

Consumer Affairs

This organization not only regulates and investigates, but in some cases enforces Federal Consumer Law. They deal with things from commercial airline rates to consumer fraud and even mailorder fraud. If your subject is a crook, or in a crooked business operating on an interstate level, chances are you will find information on them here. Locate the nearest office to you in the white pages of the telephone book.

Several years ago while investigating the owners of a very dishonest business I learned the Feds had 15,000 counts of mailorder fraud against them. Once they realized who's side I was on, they gave me all the help I needed.

Armed Services Locators

By writing to the appropriate address below, the military will locate your subject for you, should he/she be on active duty. Your request should include:
1. Name
2. Service Serial Number (usually their Social Security Number)
3. Last Known Address
4. Date of Birth
5. Last Known Rank

United States Army

Worldwide Locator Service
U.S. Army Personnel Service Support Center
Fort Benjamin Harrison, IN 46249
(317) 542-4211

United States Air Force

Air Force Military Personnel Center
Attn: Worldwide Locator
Randolph AFB
San Antonio, TX 78150
(512) 652-5774
(512) 652-5775

United States Navy

Navy Locator Service
No. 21 (if request is from a private party)
No. 36 (if request is from a military source or gov't agency)
No. 36C (if request pertains to a navy retiree)
Washington, D.C. 20370
(202) 694-3155

United States Marine Corps

Commandant of the Marine Corps
Headquarters, Marine Corps
Attn: Locator Service
Washington, D.C. 20380
(202) 694-1624 (A through E)
(202) 694-1861 (F through L)
(202) 694-1610 (M through R)
(202) 694-1913 (S through Z)

United States Coast Guard

> Coast Guard Locator Service
> Room 4502 (for enlisted personnel)
> Room 420B (for officers)
> 2100 2nd Street, S.W.
> Washington, D.C. 20593
> (202 426-8898

If your subject is a retired military or retired civil service member and receives a retirement check, contact:

> The Office of Personnel Management
> 1900 E Street, N.W.
> Washington, D.C. 20415

Social Security

The Social Security Administration has records on virtually every American. They also have records on millions of foreigners who work in this country or have since retired, and now live outside the U.S.A.

The Social Security Administration is the most secretive of all governmental agencies. Even the F.B.I. cannot get in without a court order. Even if one had a source inside, the chances of the information being up- to-date is unlikely...unless of course they are receiving payments.

However, they are willing to help a little. They will not provide you with an address but instead will forward a letter to the addressee. If you are lucky, you may just get a reply back. (Rather unlikely if your subject does not want to be found.) Mail requests to:

> Social Security Location Services
> 6401 Security Blvd.
> Baltimore, MD 21234

The following chart details how the first three digits of the Social Security Number indicates the state in which it was issued. This incidentally, is usually the state in which your subject held their first job, not necessarily their birth state.

Another note to keep in mind is that only the I.R.S. and S.S.A. index their files by

Social Security Number. For everyone else, it is against the law, and to the best of my knowledge no one else does. Examine your own card sometime; it says "not to be used for identification."

SOCIAL SECURITY INDEX OF VALID NUMBERS

001-003	New Hampshire	440-448	Oklahoma
004-007	Maine	449-467	Texas
008-009	Vermont	468-477	Minnesota
010-034	Massachusetts	478-485	Iowa
040-049	Connecticut	486-500	Missouri
035-039	Rhode Island	501-502	North Dakota
050-134	New York	503-504	South Dakota
135-158	New Jersey	505-508	Nebraska
159-211	Pennsylvania	509-515	Kansas
212-220	Maryland	516-517	Montana
221-222	Delaware	518-519	Idaho
223-231	Virginia	520	Wyoming
232-236	West Virginia	521-524	Colorado
237-246	North Carolina	525, 585	New Mexico
247-251	South Carolina	526-527	Arizona
252-260	Georgia	528-529	Utah
261-267	Florida	530	Nevada
268-302	Ohio	531-539	Washington
303-317	Indiana	540-544	Oregon
318-361	Illinois	545-573	California
362-386	Michigan	574	Alaska
387-399	Wisconsin	575-576	Hawaii
400-407	Kentucky	577-579	Dist. of Columbia
408-415	Tennessee	580	Virgin Islands
416-424	Alabama	581-585	Puerto Rico, Guam,
425-428	Mississippi		American Samoa,
429-432	Arkansas		Philippine Islands
433-439	Louisiana	700-729	Railroad

INVALID SOCIAL SECURITY NUMBERS

1. Three or more leading zeros
2. Ending in 4 zeros
3. Leading numbers 73 through 79
4. Leading number 6 or 8
5. Leading number of 9 is suspect, very few ever issued

All Social Security numbers should be nine digits. The military, however, "changed" many numbers of new recruits in the mid 1970's. Should your subject be one of these, their number will contain 10 digits with the first digit a zero. I have not seen one of these in years but there are a few around.

The Social Security number can be used in two ways. First, is the use of it to positively identify your subject. Everything from credit reports to business license applications contain or use Social Security numbers. The use of more than one by the same person should be considered suspect. The second use is employed where no other leads are available. The numbers' prefix will provide a location in which to start your search. In such cases my next step would be to search DMV records in an attempt to obtain an address. The results would then indicate my next move.

Civil Service Employees

Should your subject be a retired civil servant, try contacting the Bureau of Retirement and Insurance, of the Civil Service Commission at 1900 East "E" Street, Washington, D.C. 20415. These folks are eager to help and keep good track of retirees for pension and insurance purposes.

Civil Service employees have several associations as well. Most have locator offices and will generally provide assistance over the telephone. Consult the white pages of your local telephone book, and call the nearest office.

O.S.H.A.

O.S.H.A. has both public and private files. Cases are indexed by business name and year. Accident reports and accident investigations are generally public when complete, and vary widely in content and usefulness. Should your search lead you in this direction, do not hesitate to call them. In many cases they will provide information over the phone.

Alcohol, Tobacco and Firearms

The A.T.F. administrates and regulates any business dealing with alcohol, tobacco or firearms. They are responsible for controlling alcohol and cigarette stamps as well as issuing Federal Firearms Licenses (a license to sell guns). Most of their records are public. Generally, only their investigations are held confidential. Should you suspect your subject is involved in any of these businesses, contact your local A.T.F. office and see if they are licensed, or ever have been. They are generally very busy, but always anxious to help.

National Crime Investigation Computer

The N.C.I.C. is maintained and operated by the F.B.I. It currently contains over 25,000,000 names. The input for the N.C.I.C. comes from local, county, state and federal law enforcement agencies. Files are indexed under wanted persons, stolen vehicles, stolen license plates, stolen articles, stolen guns, stolen securities, stolen boats, criminal histories, and missing children.

Today, most police and law enforcement agencies have access to the N.C.I.C. Should you know a police officer or other law enforcement agent ask them to run the name of your subject for you. It is a crime for non- authorized persons to access the N.C.I.C., so should you have a source, keep it very confidential. It is best to ask for a criminal history to be run in the name of your subject. Should you get any "hits" go to the respective court and pull the file. It should contain new information helping you in your search. Criminal histories also provide the last known address the subject had and usually some of their most recent driving history. So if you have gotten a "hit" there is a good possibility you just found your subject. If the address is bad, run a postal check, contact neighbors, and use the appropriate local telephone directory.

U.S. Marshal's Services

The U.S. Marshal's Services is constantly looking for missing person, most of whom are fugitives. They do on occasion assist taxpayers in locating non-fugitives. Should you desire to give them a try, call the U.S. Marshal's Services at (202) 285-1100 or write them at:

> One Tysons Corner Center
> McLean, Virginia 22101.

Freedom of Information Offices

The press uses the Freedom of Information Act all the time. The catch is knowing how to ask. If the requested information is not properly identified, the government does not have to honor the request. Additionally, the law is very clear as to the format of the request. But if done properly, your request will be handled in ten days or less (that is the law). Surprisingly, a great deal of information is available under the act. In fact, anything that is not classified or does not have to do with national security is attainable. Important for us to know is that government employees' mailing addresses (including military) are available. Also the length of employment, job description, work address and salary are given. Would any of this sort of information help you if you knew your subject worked for the government?

Government Printing Office

The G.P.O. prints hundreds of thousands of publications each year. Their titles range from "Breast Feedings for the Expectant Mother" to "The Complete Text of the National Budget." They produce handsome catalogues which are published quarterly, free for the asking. One of the most significant publications available to you through the G.P.O. is the Information Book. It contains the names, addresses and phone numbers of every Federal Government Office and politician in the United States, and costs less than $20.00. Write:

Superintendent of Documents
U.S. Government Printing Office
Department 33
Washington, D.C. 20402
(202) 275-2481

Also available is the title, "Age Search Information." It describes how the census bureau records can be used for geneological research and locates.

4.6 NATIONAL

National Consumer Credit Reporting Agencies

Nearly every American above the age of 30 has an established credit history. It may not necessarily be a good one, but it is established. In order for one to buy something on credit, most creditors want to know what the applicant's credit history looks like. Chances are if they have a good track record and can afford the payments, their credit will be approved and they will get the loan. If their credit is bad, the obvious occurs.

In order for businesses, mortgage companies, banks, and financial institutions to obtain your credit history they must belong or subscribe to a Consumer Credit Reporting Agency. These agencies are strictly regulated. They process and maintain huge quantities of confidential information on you and me and make big money at it.

The largest such agency is TRW. For their customers, they provide a nifty computer printout they call the "12-Month Payment Profile," designed to show anyone's payment history for each month for a 12-month period at a glance. The document provides the subject's full name, and usually the employer. The report will also show a history of all reporting creditors. This list usually includes all credit cards, bank loans, auto loans, and other personal borrowing activity the subject has or is involved with. Only business, credit union and mortgage information is deleted. Listed for each account is the date opened, status, date of last entry made, terms of the loan, type of the loan or account, name of the creditor, account number, original amount, balance, past due amount, and payment profile.

It should be quite obvious that if you could get such a report on your subject they would probably be as good as found. The trick then is to get the report. The process is quite simple. Any business that offers it's customers credit, also subscribes to a credit reporting agency. Naturally they have access to these confidential reports. The easiest way to obtain one is to ask for one. Most businesses, however, will not provide credit reports on request, for it is against the law. Ask a friend who is in the business or owns a business to get one for you. If they do not have direct access (an account with an agency) they usually know someone who does. It's simply a matter of "knowing someone."

I should point out, if you have a written release signed by the subject, you can get the report yourself. Who would have such a release? His last landlord (very common today), the neighborhood used car dealer where they bought the car that they "skipped town" with, a local furniture store where they bought their new (and now unpaid for) furniture, and probably the neighborhood jewelry store, where they financed that special ring for their "fiancée." These businesses (if burned by your subject) will probably be most helpful in your search. If you ask for a report and tell them why you want it, they will probably provide not only the report, but a copy of the subject's credit application. With that information plus that information you already have, chances are your subject is only a few phone calls away.

TRW will also provide you a copy of your credit history. It is free if you have recently gotten turned down for credit, $6.50 if not. To obtain a copy you must provide:

1. Full Name
2. Social Security Number
3. Last Known Address
4. (A letter from the business turning you down, if applicable)

Another well known outfit is the Hooper Holms Company. This company only collects and reports negative credit information on people. They are nationwide and deal primarily with the credit card industry.

While on the subject of credit cards, should you know your subject has a certain credit or charge card, it may not hurt to contact the card company. Many have investigative and fraud divisions, looking for "missing card holders." I have often found them to be helpful and quite cooperative. Here are the addresses of a few:

CARTE BLANCHE:

3460 Wilshire Boulevard
Los Angeles, CA 90010

AMERICAN EXPRESS:

1200 Concord Pike
Wilmington, Delaware 18803

DINER'S CLUB:

10 Columbus Circle
New York, NY 10019

MOBIL OIL:

150 E. 42nd Street
New York, New York 10017

EXXON:

1251 Avenue of the Americans
New York, New York 10020

STANDARD OIL:

200 E. Randolph Drive
Chicago, Illinois 60601

SEARS: 1 Custom House Square
                                          Wilmington, Delaware 19899

J.C. PENNEY: 3801 Kennezt Pike
                                          Wilmington, Delaware 19807

Use the following form letter to initiate your correspondence with these companies. Note: Do not try calling them, you will absolutely receive no information from any credit card company over the telephone.

XYZ Credit Card Company
Investigative Services
Fraud Division

RE: David Whitefellow
    127 San Luis Way
    Placentia, CA 92345
    Account: #XYZ 12345678-910

Dear Sirs:

I (your firm) am attempting to locate Mr. Whitefellow. My search has lead me (us) to determine that he is a customer of yours in good (bad) standing. Should you know (desire to know) his current location please contact me (us) at your earliest convenience.

Thank you,

Respectfully,

(signed)
Customer Services

There is no need to explain why you are looking for your subject. They do not care so do not tell them. Use your own letterhead or that of a friend in business. Responses normally take anywhere from 4 to 6 weeks.

For more information about credit cards write:

International Association of Credit Card Investigators
1620 Grant Street
Novato, California 94947

Business Credit Reporting Agencies

Like individuals, businesses use and abuse credit. The largest and most respected Business Credit Reporting Agency is Dunn and Bradstreet. For competition, Standard, Poor's & Moody's perform the same service.

Unlike consumer credit profiles, business profiles are public. Access again, however, is only obtained through membership or subscribership. But most city libraries are members of at least one reporting agency. Another important difference is that business information is supplied by the business themselves. Also keep in mind all businesses are not listed, only those who desire to do so and apply will be on file.

As part of their services the agencies rate businesses as to their credit standing. Also provided is information about the business owners and operators, where they went to school, where they live, amount of experience in the field they are in, salaries, debt and existing lines of credit. A complete rundown on the business and its product or service is also provided. Any business purchasing on credit or borrowing money will "belong" to D & B or one of their competitors.

Executive Guide

Most libraries also have "The Business Guide to Corporate Executives." This publication is the "Who's Who of American Businesses." Listed you will find the name, address and telephone numer of the chief executives of nearly every corporation in America. (Ever wonder where newspapers get "According to an undisclosed source, Chrysler has now decided...")

Trade Associations and Societies

Choose just about any line of work, profession or business and along with it one will find an association or society. Some of the "biggies" are trade unions, Veterans, Masons, Elks, American Medical Association, and American Teacher's Association.

Every one of these organizations maintains records and information on its members. Some more than others are likely to cooperate with you. Many of the larger organizations have committees or officials designated to help locate lost or missing members. Your local library should have several directories listing such associations and societies. Call first, then write. Here are a few addresses:

ACCOUNTANTS:

Institute of Certified Public Accountants
6665 5th Avenue
New York, New York

National Association of Accountants
913 3rd Avenue
New York, New York 10022

CARPENTERS:

United Brotherhood of Carpenters and Joiners
101 Constitution Avenue
Washington, D.C.

MERCHANT SEAMEN:

National Maritime Union
Administrative Headquarters
346 West 7th Street
New York, New York

Seamen Church Institute of New York
Missing Seamen Bureau
15 State Street
New York, New York 10004

RAILROAD MEN:

Director of Retirement
Railroad Retirement Board
610 South Canal Street
Chicago, Illinois 60607

The Salvation Army

The Salvation Army has established a network to contact and locate lost souls. Their efforts are primarily directed to those on skid row and in city missions. Should you suspect your subject is in this condition, try the Salvation Army. They're listed in the white pages.

This interesting group collects information on anti-American activists. For a small contribution they will check or attempt to locate anyone. Write:

Church League of America
422 North Prospect
Wheaton, Illinois 60187

National Directory of Addresses and Phone Numbers

This publication, somewhat resembling a telephone directory, is broken down into catagories ranging from banks to hotels. It also provides a section on government, and contains thousands of hard to find government addresses and telephone numbers. There is also a section listing other directories available to the public containing similar types of information.

Interpol

Interpol, is the free world's international police department. They are headquartered in Europe, but have offices throughout the United States. For more information, call (202) 967-5685.

The MIB Networks

The Medical Information Bureau is composed of information provided by over 800 contributing and participating insurance companies. The data base is maintained in central locations and is updated hourly by its subscribers. The system provides the insurance companies with confidential medical information about you and me. At any one time over 20,000,000 people are on file.

Casualty File

Started by Hooper Holms, the casualty index contains the insurance history of over 10,000,000 Americans. Should you have ever had a claim, this index probably has a file on you.

Insurance Fraud Index

This highly secretive and highly confidential index lists virtually every American that has insurance or has applied for insurance. Listings are grouped into catagories: fire, theft, life, auto, home, business, and employment. By selecting a catagory and referencing the subject's name, you would be able to obtain the entire insurance claim and application history of that individual. Also provided would be the last known address of the insured or applicant, as the case may be.

National Change of Address Listing

Every year, 25% of the American population moves. As mentioned earlier, the post office keeps records on those who move and file a change of address card. Starting mid-1985, the postal service will be contributing this information to a central (and public) data base.

It is estimated that in five years, 95% of the American population will be on file. My personal belief is that it will be less than 25%. Most of us feel too much of our personal life is already on file. I believe most people (once learning of the system) will no longer file a change of address card.

Will you?

5.0 THE UTILITIES AND THEIR FRIENDS

Like any business, the utilities must keep track of their customer for billing purposes. They accurately maintain their customer's name, billing address, phone number and account number. Therefore, if you have one of these items, you can obtain the other information by accessing the index. Belive me, it is easier than you may think. Let's look at a few and see how to do it.

5.1 THE PHONE COMPANY

Because of the size and complexity of the nation's phone system, penetration is fairly easy. The most direct approach has already been discussed. That is the use of the directory assistance. Incidentally, there is a directory assistance for the "800" numbers; it is 1-800-555-1212. Use it next time you need a number to make a plane reservation, rent a car, call a large company, check out a bill or make a complaint.

The next approach is to use an inside source. Should you know someone who works for the phone company, or someone who knows somebody who works for the phone company, you will have your inside source. I guarantee you, someone will have access to confidential telephone company information. Your "source" once developed, will be able to provide you with **unlisted** and **unpublished numbers** (numbers not maintained in the confidential unlisted directories; for example, President Reagan's home telephone number). I have known of sources who were actually able to provide copies of the subject's actual telephone bills. Not only was I immediately able to locate my subject, but knew every long distance telephone call they made. Cross-streeting these numbers, I was able to locate a number of his friends, mother, sister, and brother. This was important information also. If my subject had suddenly disappeared, I could have easily pretexted a friend or two, and located him again.

If you have not yet developed a reliable and inexpensive source (you should not pay more than $15.00 for an unlisted or unpublished number) you will have to be a bit more creative.

Each central telephone office has a standard information disseminating system called the CNA. The CNA, or Central Names and Addresses, has computer access to all customer information (listed and unlisted) in their assigned area. Unfortunately, unpublished listings are maintained at a higher supervisory level. CNA provides customer information to other offices, linemen, installers, and other telephone companies for the asking. CNA numbers are unlisted, and are changed on a regular basis. To get a CNA number call a local business office and ask for the number to their CNA office. Tell them you are an installer (out of the area) and having difficulty in accessing "line assistance." They should either give you the CNA number or they will connect you.

Once inside, the CNA operator will be able to provide you with the address and billing name to any phone number in their area. Here is how to get it:

Ring, ring...

THEM: "Hello."

YOU: "Hi, I need one on 213-123-4568." (Most experienced linemen do not provide their name or office. You may be asked so be prepared to give it.)

THEM: "That number is listed to Arjay Miller, Los Angeles."

YOU: "Billing address?"

THEM: "Stand by.... 1 Wilshire Boulevard."

Today I have found many CNA offices can no longer provide a complete address, only the city. If so, fine. At least from the number you were able to determine the customer's name and city.

Another method is to call the number yourself. Call very early in order to wake your subject up.

Ring, ring....

THEM: "Hello"

YOU: "This is Pacific Bell, lineman #67, please hold."

   (Now, using the push buttons on the phone, push several numbers, it will not disconnect you)

YOU: "Yeah...Bill, I finally made the connection, but no voltage...(pause).... yeah.... yeah.... O.K., hold on."

   Push the same buttons again, and state to your subject:

YOU: "Excuse me, we have a down trunk line. What is your customer address and area code?

If it is not immediately provided, insist that their line is the only line thus reconnected and in order to identify and reconnect the others you must first identify their location.

I have gone so far as to ask them where they work, "so I may call them" and "test" that number. I sometimes ask them their name also if I am uncertain of their identity.

Also available to you is Customer Service. By either calling 411, or 1-area code (where you suspect your subject is)-555-1212, call the customer service billing office and try one of these approaches:

Ring, ring....

YOU: "Hello, this is John from customer service in Reno, Nevada. How are you today? How is the weather, cold I bet...Hey, listen. I have a customer here claiming to have $30.00 in reversed charges to (213) 123-4567, and claims that they are not his. Could you check out this number and see if you have a listing for it...(then partly cupping the mouthpiece of the phone)..."Yes, sir...I am sorry, we are checking on it right now..."

THEM: "Yes, I show it is listed to an Arjay Miller at 1 Wilshire Blvd., Los Angeles. Is that all you need?....."

#2: Ring, ring....

YOU: "Hi, this is John from customer service in Reno, Nevada. I have a customer (state subject's name) here attempting to establish service and for the life of me I cannot seem to show prior service with you guys...do you show a listing?"

They will probably ask what the previous telephone number and address were; make them up. Just ensure the prefix you give matches the area you are calling.

THEM: "That's funny. I don't show a listing either. The only one I have is (213) 123-4567, at 1 Wilshire Blvd. Sorry."

Customer service will also provide copies of bills. In order to obtain someone else's bill, call customer service and state that you lost "**your**" bill (obviously you give them the name of the person you are trying to locate, not your own name).

They will only send it to the address listed on the bill, so you must tell them you have moved or ask them to mail it to your office since "kids steal mail in my neighborhood."

5.2 GAS AND ELECTRIC COMPANIES

Like the phone companies, these folks can be gagged also. They are easily accessed and usually more than anxious to cooperate. Apply some of the gags already demonstrated or make up your own. Remember, most residential gas and electric meters have the customer's name on the tag attached to the meter. So if you have the address, chances are you can get the customer's name.

The best approach is to tell the company that you have not received a bill in two months...then ask them what address they are mailing it to. If they ask you first, make one up. Then when they give you the real one, tell them, "No wonder you guys are messed up; you do not even know where I live!"

Any variation of this approach will work.

5.3 WATER AND TRASH

These folks are real easy to work. Just about any approach will work with either of them. I have even called and told them I was looking for somebody and asked if he was a customer. They said "Yes," and gave me the address.

I suggest you try customer service. State you are a bill collector for them and are in the field. Provide them your subject's name and tell them the address does not check out; ask them to verify it. They will give you the correct address. Ask them for the phone number, also.

5.4 EMPLOYER

If you are able to locate a current or previous employer, ask to speak to your subject's immediate supervisor. Today, because of the law and courts, most employers will only verify the information you already have. Be patient and friendly. Try this:

YOU: "Maybe if I describe the job we are considering placing Arjay in, you can better help me. Is he good with people?"

THEM: "Oh yeah... he knew everybody here. I think Susan, my secretary, and he still stay in touch; hold on let me ask her."

And so it goes. Do not be afraid to ask questions. Be sure to also ask questions that provide you some legitimacy. As a rule of thumb, the bigger the company the harder it is to get information. If it takes ten telephone calls to get someone who will talk, do it. Be persistent.

Sometimes, direct approach is the best. Simply state you are an old friend and are trying to track him/her down. If you know enough about your subject, you should be able to field any questions somebody will throw at you.

THEM: "Oh yeah... I did not know he went to UCLA. What year?"

YOU: "Graduated 1975, School of Medicine. You mean he never told you about...etc. etc." "How about you Where did you go to school?..."

A friendly and direct approach is sometimes the best.

Friends and Relatives

These folks should be approached as if you are an old friend or employer. Same rules apply. Be friendly, talk it up, and do not be bashful. If they do not know where your subject is or how to reach them, ask if they know of someone who does. Around tax time, state you (the employer) have a W-2 form, but no address to mail it to. Be creative and be prepared to answer any question they may throw at you.

Banks

Banks are tough. They accept any information (or money) you give them, but hate to give it out. Knowing this, I usually like to trade information with them. Either about my subject or someone else they may be looking for. Very few people in the bank will be able to handle this type of offer, so be sure you pitch it to the right person, and not get pitched out the door instead!

Banks, however, as a matter of practice will verify information. They will also give information on whether a check of a certain size will "clear" against an account. This may be important information should you be looking for someone who owes you money.

In other words, should you know where your subject banks, you could call stating:

YOU: This is the Hampton Gallery. We are about to receive a check from a Mr. XYZ (subject's name) and he informs that he has an account with you. Could you verify that please?"

THEM: "Sure, please hold... yes. Mr. XYZ does have a checking account here."

YOU: "Would a six figure check clear today?"

THEM: "Yes, it would."

YOU: "Thank you."

The following is a list of terms used to indicate the balance in a bank account. Most credit rating bureaus also use this method of converting dollars into a low, medium and high code.

LOW 1	$1.00 - $3.99
LOW 2	$10.00 - $39.00
LOW 3	$100.00 - $399.99
LOW 4	$1000.00 - $3,999.99
LOW 5	$10,000.00 - $39,999.99
MEDIUM 1	$4.00 - $6.99
MEDIUM 2	$40.00 - $69.99
MEDIUM 3	$400.00 - $699.99
MEDIUM 4	$4,000.00 - $6,999.99
MEDIUM 5	$40,000.00 - $69,999.99
HIGH 1	$7.00 - $9.99
HIGH 2	$70.00 - $99.99
HIGH 3	$700.00 - $999.99
HIGH 4	$7,000.00 - $9,999.99
HIGH 5	$70,000.00 - $99,999.99

If you are not sure what the person reporting to you is saying always verify it.

The best opener when dealing with a bank is to ask, "Will you please verify an address for me?" Give them the last known address you have and three times out of four if they have a newer one, they will automatically give it to you. The following is the formal terminology given by banks, finance companies and some credit unions when discribing their ratings.

CREDIT TERMINOLOGY

Opened 10 of 84	——Means opened the account or loan October,1984
High of $5,000	——Means the highest credit granted was $5,000
Payments of $50	——May just say payments 24 at 35 = 24 months at $35
10 - 15 Day	——Means the debtor was sent ten 15-day late notices
Slow Pay	——Payments were 30 days or more late several times
Paid As Agreed	——Payments made according to contract terms

ALWAYS ask additional questions if you need more information than the person you are talking to has volunteered. If a loan was involved ask if it was secured or unsecured, co-signed or unco-signed, when the debtor first established credit with their company or got their first loan. These are all acceptable and very likely to be answered.

5.5 LANDLORDS AND NEIGHBORS

To the private investigator, these people have to be just about our best friends. The working of these highly informative sources is called conducting an "activity check." There are a number of ways to go about it. Some of the pretexts already discussed will work, but there are a few sure fire ones I will walk you through.

The first is the call for jury duty (see following page). Approach the neighbor or landlord, and inform them that your subject has not responded by mail. They may immediately state:

"He and his wife moved out a month ago..don't know where thought...

Press the issue. State locating him will be no problem and attempt to obtain the answers on your questionnaire. When that is accomplished, ask how **he** suggests you locate your subject. Go to the next neighbor and do the same. Collect as much information as you can, and follow up on all leads.

Landlords are easy, also. Give them the same pitch. They, however, *do know* where your subject moved to because they sent the deposit check there. If they do not provide it, ask to see the Application To Rent. Like a credit application, it contains untold secrets about your subject. From it alone, chances are your subject is only a few phone calls away.

Incidently, in the case of a "rent jumper," the application probably contains phony information. In that case, you are going to have to use another approach.

For landlords who will not cooperate, call them by phone and state:

YOU: "Hi, this is Arjay Miller, down at Camera World, I have been trying to reach (subject's name) for two months, and it looks like they have moved; do you have their forwarding address?"

THEM: "No, I am sorry, I cannot give that out," or, "They asked that I not give it out."

YOU: "O.K., hold on...(papers russeled)well it looks like these are original wedding photos...let me see, yeah here is one of Mrs. (subject's name)...man these negative are old too...they must be originals."

THEM: "Ok, Ok. But do not tell them I gave you their address. There are alot of people looking for them, okay?"

If the party you are speaking with states, "Mail the photos to us and we will forward them," you say:

YOU: "Sure.... That will be $85.59, C.O.D. I will have one of my guys bring them out tomorrow."

Depending on how much you know about your subject, a direct approach might be best. Depending on your reason for looking for someone, others may be looking for them also. If you can determine who the others are, they will be more than anxious to exchange information and assist you.

1. Subject's Educational Background:
   When:
   Where:

2. What was his major?

3. How long did he live at this address?

4. Would he be familiar with the laws in your state?

5. Are his parents still living?

6. Where do they live?

7. Is he married?

8. Does he have any children?

9. Are they in school?

10. Was he employed?
    Where:
    For how long:
    Did what:

11. Has he ever been arrested or convicted?
    Why:
    Where:

12. Was he ever involved in a civil suit?

14. Hobbies, sports, past-times?

15. Did he have any friends?
    Who:
    Where:

16. Would he be fit for jury duty?

17. Was he politically active?

18. Was he a member of a union?

19. Did he own a business?

20. Would he be fair and unbiased as a juror?

6.0 OUTSIDE HELP

One would think a private investigator would be the first person one should turn to when attempting to locate someone. As a private investigator myself, my response to that notion is not what you would expect. Most private investigators do "locates" as I do. You will find however, our effectiveness and degree of professionalism varies widely. The problem is, you are paying someone else for something you could probably do better. Do not get me wrong; I know a few investigators who are incredible. But, if you are working within budget constraints, I recommend you seek the services of a private investigator only if you have exhausted everything I have shown you so far. Only then might one be of help.

For businesses, on the other hand, an investigation firm is the only way to go. Most businesses do not have enough time to chase people down, and should instead stick to the business they know best, their own.

Over the years, I have come across a handful of helpful outside sources, a list of which follows. Keep in mind, however, with the exception of the books mentioned, these sources are businesses and will charge a fee.

Equifax Services

This company is nationwide. Equifax is the largest consumer investigation agency in the world, with over 10,000 investigators. Their parent company is the Retail Credit Company, headquartered in Atlanta, Georgia. With gross sales of over $1,000,000,000 a year, you can bet they are a powerful influence in the industry. You can either contact a local office or write:

> Retail Credit Company
> P.O. Box 4081
> Atlanta, Georgia 30302

Vehicle Operator Searches (VOS)

These folks can provide data on virtually every driver, traffic ticket and accident in the United States.

> P.O. Box 15334
> Sacramento, California 95813
> (916) 451-8475.

Executive Search Corporation

They perform searches for all of the following: courts, property, corporations, real property, DMV, telephone, and voter's registration. Most searches are under $50.00.

> 29 West Thomas Road
> Phoenix, Arizona 85013
> (800) 528-6179.

IRSC

They offer overnight searches for under $25.00. Services include courts, real property, DMV and Nation-wide Postal Locates (includes 135,000,000 names). Their real asset is that they are computerized and subscribers with computers can access their files directly.

3777 North Harbor Boulevard
Fullerton, California 92635
(800) 321-2278.

Investigative News

A monthly newsletter providing its readers with up-to-date information on methods, techniques, books, and products used in the industry. Also reviews the latest laws and court decisions nation-wide affecting the investigation business and those in it. A great reference source.

Investigative News
407 West Santa Clara Avenue, Suite #1
Santa Ana, California 92706

The Assignment Center

A referral service for private investigators, security companies, crime labs, process servers, forensic labs, and toxicologists.

(800) 237-3833
(813) 879-8580 (in Florida)

Here are a few organizations that maintain locating assistance offices:

American Legion	(317) 635-8411
ELKS	(312) 477-2750
Disabled American Veterans	(606) 441-7300
MOOSE	(312) 859-2000
VFW	(816) 756-3390
Information Industry Association	(608) 262-2762

Clipping Services

These folks read everything published or printed and clip out articles. They file them by topic, subject, or name and offer them for sale to their subscribers. If your subject was part of some significant event or catastrophe (sinking of the Titanic) you may want to see if a clipping service is of any help. Here are a few:

Bacon's	(800) 621-0561
Burrelle's Press	(800) 631-1160
Lace	(800) 528-8226
New York	(800) 631-1160

BOOKS

National Directory of Addresses and Telephone Numbers

850 Third Avenue
New York, New York 10022.

This book lists every 800 number, member of government (including the President; his office telephone number is (202) 456-1414), bank, law firm, trade union, airline, and accountant. It is a terrific tool, every investigative reporter I know has one.

Confidential Information Sources, Public and Private

By John M. Carroll, Security World Publication Co., Inc.
Library of Congress #74-20177

Butterworth Inc.,
10 Tower Office Park
Woburn, Massachusetts 01801

Names and Numbers

By Rod Norland
John Wiley & Sons, Inc., Publisher
New York, New York

7.0 MISSING CHILDREN

Locating missing children is a science of its own. In my opinion, the approach to the problem is prevention. For several dollars, parents can buy a "do-it-yourself" finger printing kit and in a matter of minutes fingerprint their children. All police stations and many schools now will fingerprint children for no charge. Without exception, I recommend your children wear identification tags. I recently saw cloth tags sewn into a child's clothes; a good idea you may want to copy. If a national effort was made in this direction, all of our children would be safer.

Education is also essential. Many parents have trained their children to respond to adults only if they know the "password." This concept is fun for children and easy to use. The child is taught never to talk to or go with a stranger, no matter what they might say - unless they give the "password." The password should actually be two words somewhat unrelated to each other. For example, Baby-Train, Rocket-House, or Peanut Butter-Soap.

The reason for this is to prevent strangers from accidently saying the password. The child should also be taught to challenge any stranger who does not use the password. By doing so, the stranger will be put on immediate notice that both the child and the parent have prepared for such a situation and the child will not be an easy snatch.

Children should also know their name, address, and telephone number. By doing so, they can identify themselves if they lose their identification. If they are lost, they can be returned that much easier. Lastly, children should know what kidnapping is and what it means. They should also know how to say it. Have you ever wondered how an eleven year old child who has been gone from his/her parents for six years, never realized it was kidnapped? By some incredible fluke, the child is then determined to have been kidnapped and is returned to their rightful parents. Research has shown in many cases, the child never realized that they were kidnapped. The abductor told (taught) the child, "Changing parents is normal and all children do it."

If the child is trained properly, at some point it will realize it was kidnapped and attempt to get away.

Once gone, children leave few traces. They have no social security number, driver's license, job, bank account, or credit cards. Thus much like the scene of a murder, the location where the event took place holds the most clues. Most adults are not considered missing until 48 to 72 hours have elapsed. For children, that length of time may only be minutes, depending on their age, and circumstances. Once the child is considered actually missing, immediate action must be taken. The authorities must be notified and a search begun.

Should this ever happen to you, immediately go to the location the child was last seen. Look not only for the child but examine the surrounding areas. Write down license plate numbers, people's names and addresses. Ask plenty of questions and do not hesitate to question strangers, particularly those who appear to have been at the scene for some time (picnicers, road crews, etc.).

Write down their names and phone numbers so you may contact them at a later date. Be thorough, and try not to panic. The child needs every ounce of composure you have.

Once the authorities arrive, cooperate with them. Be prepared to provide a complete description including the size and make of shoes and other pieces of clothing. Police will also want a very recent photograph of the child, preferrably a closeup of their face and/or a full body shot. The very least any parent should have is a recent photograph of the face. Once the police have taken charge, the only thing left to do is wait.

Should you desire more information on the subject of missing children, contact any one of the following organizations. Your yellow and white pages should provide other groups as well.

National Missing Children Hotline
(800) 843-5678

Child Find, Inc.
P.O. Box 277
New Paltz, NY 12561
(800) 431-5005

National Center for Missing and Exploited Children
1835 K Street N.W. Suite 700
Washington D.C. 20006
(206) 634-9821

Find the Children
11811 W. Olympic Blvd.
Los Angeles, CA 90064
(213) 477-6721

National Child Identification Center, Inc.
P.O. Box 3068 A
Albuquerque, New Mexico 87190
(800) 222-4453

You may also want to get the Directory of Runaway Houses: National Youth Alternatives Project: 1346 Connecticut Avenue, Washington, D.C. 20036. Here are a few organizations from their directory.

National Runaway Hotline
Continental United States
(800) 621-4000
(Illinois only: (800) 972-6004)

North Virginia Hotline
Arlington 22210
(703) 527-4077

Parental Stress Service Hotline
Chicago, IL 60605
(312) 463-0390

Cleveland Community Information Service Hotline
Cleveland, OH 44115
(216) 696-4262

Parental Stress Service, Inc. Hotline
Oakland, CA 94610
(415) 655-3535

Salvation Army Transient Lodge Hotline
San Antonio, TX 78202
(512) 226-2291

Contact Hotline
St. Louis, MO 63117
(3145) 725-3022

D.C. Hotline
Washington, D.C. 20005
(202) 462-6690

Parents Anonymous Hotline
Continental United States
(800) 421-0353
California only: (800) 352-0353

Metro-Help Hotline
Chicago, IL 60614
(312) 929-5150

Operation Peace of Mind
Continental United States
(800) 231-6946
Texas only (800) 392-3352

Crisis Hotline of Houston
Houston, TX 77210
(713) 228-1505

Philadelphia Hotline
Philadelphia 19151
(215) 879-4402

Crisis Center Hotline
San Antonio, TX 78228
(512) 227-4357

Alum Rock Counseling Hotline
San Jose, CA 95127
(408) 251-4422

Autumn House Hotline
Tacson, AZ 85705
(602) 623-6793

The United States Department of State can conduct a "welfare and whereabouts" search to locate a child and determine the physical condition of the child if he or she has been taken from the country. Such requests should be made to the Office of Citizen Consular Services, Room 4811, Department of State, Washington, D.C. 20520, or by telephone at (202) 632- 3444.

AS A PARENT YOU SHOULD:

1. Know your child's friends,

2. Never leave your child unattended,

3. Never leave young children to supervise other children,

4. Teach your child to use the telephone. Ensure they know how to use "0" for the operator and "911" for "help".

5. Teach your children *your* first and last name. Ensure they know their home address and phone numbers, (and can dial the number).

6. Teach your children that they can say NO to adults.

7. Teach each child a secret password to be used to identify friendly adults; for example should someone else pick them up at school.

8. Request your child's school to call you when your child is absent.

9. Teach them to never talk to strangers.

10. Teach them never to accept gifts or rides from strangers.

11. Teach them that no one (uncle, grandparent, friends, etc) have the right to touch them in a way they do not like.

12. Know where your children are at all times, even if they are only next door.

13. Know who they are with at all times.

14. Never put the child's name on the outside of their clothing. This often gives the abductor a "friendly edge".

15. Allow your children to talk to you, allow them to openly discuss their day's activites.

16. Be sensitive to changes in their moods and attitudes.

17. Have a set plan for the child as to what they should do, if lost or abducted. Rehearse the plan.

18. Set boundaries for them in which to play.

19. Teach them to report all suspicious people to you.

20. Know your children's babysitters friends, parents, and teachers.

21. Know your neighbors and establish "safehouses" in your neighborhood.

22. Fingerprint your children and keep current identification records on them.

23. Use common sense and never take chances.

YOUR CHILD'S IDENTIFICATION

Package Should Include:

1. A complete set of fingerprints, done at home or professionally.

2. Current dental records, to include x-rays.

3. Current color photograph (should be taken at least once a year) facial and full body.

4. Birth certificate.

5. Parental information.

6. Custody information, include full information on other parent, especially their current address.

7. Medical records and blood type.

8. Physical description to include height, weight, eye and hair color, clothe and shoe size.

Keep your child's indentification in a safe and accessable place. A fireproof file box will due best. A duplicate package may be kept in a safety deposit box or with another family member.

SOME OTHER IDEAS!

1. For very young children, an identification bracelet with name, address and telephone number engraved on it might be helpful.

2. Tell your children, never to go with your ex-spouse unless you have first approved it.

3. Have your child telephone you if they arrive at home when you are not there, and visa-versa.

8.0 ADOPTION RECORDS

For obvious investigative reasons adoption records are of particular interest. But for the adoptee the search is often personal and takes on special meaning. For them the search of ones roots can be mere curiosity or it can be a life fulfilling goal. Regardless, most adoptees find their ancestorial past unaccessable. Sealed and secured by the court in which the adoption took place, these records are held sacred never to be reviewed by those who most desire to see them.

At the time the adoption takes place a new birth certificate is issued. Hospital records are changed to reflect the "new birth" and other documents are sealed in the case file. The obvious intention is to protect all three parties—the birth parents, the adoptive parents, and of course the child. In doing so, however, searching adult adoptees find a hopeless tangle of red tape and frustration. With few exceptions these records are never made available. For those that are, the payoff can be exhilarating.

To effect such a search the first place to start is with the adoptive parents. They should be able to provide some detail as to the arrangements at the time of adoption. Thorough investigation often reveals birth parent information available no where else. Diaries, photo albums and other personal documents and papers will help trace the family back to the time of adoption. Also important is the interviewing of old family friends and relatives. Often these people know "the secret" and will provide information if asked properly.

From my point of view the investigation begins, however, once the names of the birth parents are found. I have conducted several of these types of investigations with only limited success. The difficulty stems as a result of time. Considering that in most cases, the search begins twenty or more years after the adoption, we normally find records obscure and incomplete. Generally, determining the location of the birth parents at the time of the adoption is no problem. Usually local public records will provide this information. The problem begins, however, when they begin to move. Postal records generally are of no help nor are they quick to locate methods. These investigations require field work, long hours and patience.

No matter what information you start with, follow the methods and procedures discussed earlier. They are fool-proof, and if followed to the letter, will yield success.

For those who are interested, I have provided on the following pages a quick review of adoption record policies by State and a list of government offices regulating adoption and adoption records. Also is a list of private agencies.★ Attorneys specialize in this field. If interested, consult your local Bar Association. Their telephone number can be found in the yellow pages.

★Courtesy People Finders Magazine.

Open/Closed Adoption Records Status by State

State	Jurisdiction	Records Open/Closed	Birth Cert. available at age of majority	Age of maturity
Alabama	Probate Court	Open★	Y	19
Alaska	Superior Court	Closed	N	18
Arizona	Superior Court	Closed	N	18
Arkansas	Probate Court	Closed	N	18
California	Superior Court	Closed	N	18
Colorado	District Court	Closed	N	18-21
Connecticut	Probate/Juvenile	Closed	N	18
Delaware	Superior/Orphans	Closed	N	18
D.C.	General Sessions	Closed	N	18
Florida	Circuit Court	Closed	N	18
Georgia	Superior Court	Closed	N	18
Hawaii	Family Court	Closed	N	18
Idaho	Magistrate/Probate	Closed	N	—
Illinois	Circuit Court	Closed	N	18
Indiana	(See notes)	Closed	N	18
Iowa	District Court	Closed	N	18
Kansas	District Court	Open	Y	18
Kentucky	Circuit Court	Closed	N	18
Louisiana	District/Juvenile	Closed	N	18
Maine	Probate Court	Closed	Y	18
Maryland	(See notes)	Closed★★	N	18
Massachusettes	Probate Court	Closed	N	—
Michigan	Probate Court	Closed	N	—
Minnesota	Juvenile/District	Closed	N	21
Mississippi	Chancery Court	Closed	N	18-21
Missouri	Circuit Court	Closed	N	18
Montana	District/Tribal	Closed	N	18
Nebraska	County Court	Closed	N	18
Nevada	District Court	Closed	N	18
New Hampshire	Probate Court	Closed	N	18
New Jersey	(See notes)	Closed★★★	—	—
New Mexico	District Court	Closed	N	18
New York	(See notes)	Closed	N	18
N. Carolina	Superior Court	Closed	N	18
N. Dakota	District/Probate	Closed	N	18-21
Ohio	Probate Court	Closed	Y★★★★★	18
Oklahoma	(See notes)	Closed	N	18
Oregon	Circuit Court	Closed	N	18
Rhode Island	Family/Probate	Closed	N	18
S. Carolina	Family Court	Closed★★★★	N	18
S. Dakota	Circuit Court	Closed	N	18
Tennessee	(See notes)	Closed	N	18
Texas	(See notes)	Closed	N	—
Utah	District Court	Closed	N	18
Vermont	Probate Court	Closed	N	18
Virginia	Circuit Court	Closed	N	18
Washington	Superior Court	Closed	N	18
W. Virginia	Circuit/Juvenile	Closed	N	18
Wisconsin	Circuit Court	Closed	N	18
Wyoming	District Court	Closed	N	19

Notes: Open Records

★ Alabama adoption records open when adoptee reaches age of 19, excluding names of natural parents.

★★ Maryland adoption records closed except in some cases finalized prior to 7/1/47.

★★★ New Jersey adoption records closed except for cases finalized prior to 1940-1941.

★★★★ South Carolina adoption records closed except for cases finalized prior to 2/3/64.

★★★★★ Ohio birth certificates available to those over 18 for adoptions finalized prior to 1964.

JURISDICTION

Indiana - Superior, Probate or County Court with Probate Jurisdiction

Maryland - Chancely or Circuit or any court in the city of Baltimore having eguity jurisdiction

New Jersey - Domestic Relations Court, Superior Court, County Court or Juvenile Court

New York - Surrogates Court, Family Court and Supreme Court

Oklahoma - Children's Court, County Court or District Court

Tennessee - Probate Court, Circuit Court or Court of Chancery

Texas - District Court, Circuit Court or Court of Chancery

State Capitol Office and Agencies with Jurisdiction over Adoptions

ALABAMA

State Capitol
Montgomery, Alabama 36130
(205) 832-6011

Bureau of Family and
    Children's Services
State Department of Pensions
    & Security
64 North Union Street
Montgomery, Alabama 36130

ALASKA

State Capitol
120 4th Street
Juneau, Alaska 99881
(907) 465-2111

Department of Health & Social
    Services
ouch H-05
Juneau, Alaska 99881

ARIZONA

State Capitol
1700 West Washington Street
Phoenix, Arizona 85007
(602) 271-4900

Department of Economic
    Security
Administration for Children,
    Youth and Families
P.O. Box 6123
1400 West Washington Street
Phoenix, Arizona 85005

ARKANSAS

State Capitol
5th and Woodland
Little Rock, Arkansas 72201
(501) 371-3000

Department of Human
    Services
Division of Social Services
Adoption Services
P.O. Box 1437
Little Rock, Arkansas 72203

CALIFORNIA

State Capitol
10th and L Streets
Sacramento, California 95814
(916) 445-4711

Department of Social Services
Adoption Branch
744 "P" Street
Sacramento, California 95814

COLORADO

State Capitol
200 East Colfax Avenue
Denver, Colorado 80203
(303) 892-9911

Department of Social Services
Post Adoption Services
1575 Sherman Street
Denver, Colorado 80203

CONNECTICUT

State Capitol
210 Capitol Ave.
Hartford, Connecticut 06115
(203) 5660-2211

Department of Children &
    Youth Services
Adoption Services
Adoption Resource Exchange
170 Sigourney Street
Hartford, Connecticut 06105

DELAWARE

State Capitol
Dover, Delaware 19901
(302) 678-4000

Division of Social Services
Department of Health &
    Social Services
P.O. Box 309
Wilmington, Delaware 19899

DISTRICT OF COLUMBIA

District Building
14th and "E" Streets, N.W.
Washington, D.C. 20004
(202) 628-6000

Bureau of Family Services
Social Rehabilitation
    Administration
122 "C" Street N.W.
Washington, D.C. 20001

FLORIDA

The Capitol
Tallahassee, Florida 32304
(905) 488-1234

Department of Health and
    Rehabilitative Services
1317 Winewood Boulevard
Tallahassee, Florida 32301

GEORGIA

State Capitol
Capitol Square, S.W.
Atlanta, Georgia 30334
(404) 656-2000

Division of Social Services
Department of Human
    Resources
618 Ponce de Leon
    Avenue, N.E.
Atlanta, Georgia 30334

HAWAII

State Capitol
415 South Beretania Street
Honolulu, Hawaii 96813
(808) 548-2211

Department of Social Services
    and Housing
P.O. Box 339
Honolulu, Hawaii 96809

IDAHO

Statehouse
700 West Jefferson Street
Boise, Idaho 83720
(208) 384-2411

Department of Health
    and Welfare
Statehouse
Boise, Idaho 83720

ILLINOIS

State Capitol
Springfield, Illinois 62706
(217) 782-2000

Department of Children
    & Family Services
1 North Old State
    Capitol Plaza
Springfield, Illinois 62706

INDIANA

State House
200 West Washington
    Street
Indianapolis, Indiana 46204
(317) 633-4000

Social Services Division
State Department of Public
    Welfare
141 South Meridian Street
Indianapolis, Indiana 46225

IOWA

Capitol Building
100 East Grand Avenue
Des Moines, Iowa 50319
(505) 281-5011

Iowa Department of Social
    Services
Bureau of Children's Services
Division of Community
    Programs
Hoover Building
Des Moines, Iowa 50319

KANSAS

State House
10th and Harrison Streets
Topeka, Kansas 66612
(913) 296-0111

Department of Social and
    Rehabilitative Services
Division of Children and Youth
2700 West 6th Street
Topeka, Kansas 66606

KENTUCKY

State Capitol
Frankfort, Kentucky 40601
(502) 564-2500

Bureau for Social Services
Department of Human
    Resources
275 East Main Street,
    6th Floor West
Frankfort, Kentucky 40601

LOUISIANA

State Capitol
900 Riverside, North
Baton Rouge, Louisiana 70804
(504) 389-6601

Office of Human Development
Adoption Program
333 Laurel, Room 704
Baton rouge, Louisiana 70801

MAINE

State House
Augusta, Maine 04333

Department of Human
    Services
221 State Street
Augusta, Maine 04333

MARYLAND

State House
State Circle
Annapolis, Maryland 21404
(301) 267-0100

Department of Human
    Resources
Social Services Administration
11 South Street
Baltimore, Maryland 21202

MASSACHUSETTS

State House
Beacon Street
Boston, Massachusetts 02133
(617) 727-2121

Department of Social Services
150 Causeway Street
Boston, Massachusetts 02114

MICHIGAN

Capitol Building
Lansing, Michigan 48933
(517) 373-1837

Department of Social Services
300 South Capitol Avenue
Post Office Box 30037
Lansing, Michigan 48909

MINNESOTA

State Capitol
Aurora Avenue and
    Park Street
St. Paul, Minnesota 55155
(612) 296-6013

Department of Public Welfare
Centennial Office Building
St. Paul, Minnesota 55155

MISSISSIPPI

New Capitol Building
Jackson, Mississippi 39205
(601) 354-7011

Department of Public Welfare
515 East Amite Street
Jackson, Mississippi 39205

MISSOURI

State Capitol
Jefferson City, Missouri 65101
(314) 751-2151

Division of Family Services
Department of Social Services
P.O. Box 88
Jefferson City, Missouri 65103

MONTANA

Capitol Building
Helena, Montana 59601
(406) 449-2511

Social Services Bureau
Department of Social and
    Rehabilitative Services
111 Sanders
Helena, Montana 59601

NEBRASKA

State Capitol
1445 K Street
Lincoln, Nebraska 68509
(402) 471-2311

Department of Public Welfare
Division of Social Services
P.O. Box 95026
Lincoln, Nebraska 68509

NEVADA

State Capitol
Carson City, Nevada 89710
(702) 885-5000

Welfare Division
Department of Human
    Resources
251 Jeanell Drive
Capitol Mall Complex
Carson City, Nevada 89710

NEW HAMPSHIRE

State House
107 North Main Street
Concord,
New Hampshire 03301
(603) 271-1110

Bureau of Child and Family
    Services
State Department of Health
    and Welfare
Hazen Drive
Concord,
New Hampshire 03301

NEW JERSEY

State House
Trenton, New Jersey 08625
(609) 292-2121

Division of Youth and Family
    Services
Department of Institutions
    and Agencies
P.O. Box 510
Trenton, New Jersey 08625

NEW MEXICO

State Capitol
Santa Fe, New Mexico 87501
(505) 827-4011

Human Services Department
Social Services Division
Adoption Services
P.O. Box 2348
Santa Fe, New Mexico 87503

NEW YORK STATE

State Capitol
Albany, New York 12224
(518) 474-2121

Division of Services
New York State Department
    of Social Services
40 North Pearl Street
Albany, New York 12243

NORTH CAROLINA

State Capitol
Raleigh, North Carolina 27611
(919) 829-1110

Children's Services Branch
Division of Social Services
325 North Salisbury Street
Raleigh, North Carolina 27611

NORTH DAKOTA

State Capitol
Bismarck, North Dakota 58505
(701) 224-2000

Children and Family Services
Russel Building
Box 7
Bismarck, North Dakota 58505

OHIO

State House
Broad and High Streets
Columbus, Ohio 43215
(614) 466-2000

Department of Public Welfare
Division of Social Services
30 East Broad Street,
30th Floor
Columbus, Ohio 43215

OKLAHOMA

State Capitol
2302 Lincoln Boulevard
Oklahoma City,
Oklahoma 73105
(405) 521-2011

Division of Child Welfare
Department of Human
    Services
P.O. Box 25352
Oklahoma City,
Oklahoma 73125

OREGON

State Capitol
Salem, Oregon 97310
(503) 378-3131

Adoption Services
Department of Human
    Resources
Children's Services Division
198 Commercial Street, S.E.
Salem, Oregon 97310

RHODE ISLAND

State House
82 Smith Street
Providence,
Rhode Island 02903
(401) 277-2000

Department for Children and
    Their Families
610 Mt. Pleasant Avenue
Providence,
Rhode Island 02908

SOUTH CAROLINA

State House
Columbia,
South Carolina 29211
(803) 758-0221

The Children's Bureau of
    South Carolina
Building D
800 Dutch Square Boulevard
Columbia,
South Carolina 29221

SOUTH DAKOTA

Capitol Building
Pierre, South Dakota 57501
(605) 224-3011

Department of Social Services
Richard F. Kneip Building
Pierre, South Dakota 57501

TENNESSEE

State Capitol
Nashville, Tennessee 37219
(615) 741-3011

Department of Human
    Services
111-19 7th Avenue North
Nashville, Tennessee 37203

TEXAS

State Capitol
Austin, Texas 78711
(512) 475-2323

Department of Human
    Resources
706 Bannister Lane
P.O. Box 2960
Austin, Texas 78769

UTAH

State Capitol
Salt Lake City, Utah 84114
(801) 533-4000

Division of Family Services
Department of Social Services
150 West North Temple
Salt Lake City, Utah 04103

VERMONT

State House
State Street
Montpelier, Vermont 05602
(802) 828-1110

Agency of Human Services
Department of Social and
    Rehabilitation Services
103 South Main Street
Waterbury, Vermont 05676

VIRGINIA

State Capitol
Capitol Square
Richmond, Virginia 23219
(804) 786-0000

Division of Social Services
Department of Welfare
8007 Discovery Drive
Richmond, Virginia 23288

WASHINGTON

State Capitol
Olympia, Washington 98504
(206) 753-5000

Department of Social and
    Health Services
Bureau of Children's Services
Office Building 2
Olympia, Washington 98504

WEST VIRGINIA

1800 Kanawha Boulevard,
    East
Charleston,
West Virginia 25305
(304) 348-3456

Department of Welfare
1900 Washington Street, East
Charleston,
West Virginia 25305

WISCONSIN

State Capitol
Capitol Square
Madison, Wisconsin 53702
(608) 266-2211

Division of Community
    Services
Department of Health and
    Social Services
1 West Wilson Street
Madison, Wisconsin 53702

WYOMING

State Capitol
Capitol Avenue at 24th Street
Cheyenne, Wyoming 82201
(307) 777-7220

Division of Public Assistance
    and Social Services
Hathaway Building
Cheyenne, Wyoming 82002

The following is only a partial list of sources with information about adoption and adoption research. Should you find nothing close to home, consult a local telephone directory.

ALASKA

Adoptees Liberty Movement
   Assn. ALMA Chapter
Box 372
Glennallen AK 99588

Concerned United
   Birthparents
Rep. Jana Shedlock
7105 Shooreson Circle
Anchorage AK 99504

ALABAMA

Adoptees Liberty Movement
   Assn. ALMA Chapter
Box 55063
Birmingham AL 35255

Concern United Birthparents
CUB Rep. Virginia Womack
Rte. 3 Box 579
Trussville, AL 35173

Search Line of Texas Chapter
3902 1/2 20th St. N.E.
Tuscaloosa AL 35404

ARKANSAS

Searchline
Rt. 5 Box 29-B
Huntsville AR 72740

ARIZONA

Adoptees Liberty Movement
   Assn. ALMA Chapter
Box 25966
Tempe AZ 85282

Parents and Adoptees Uplifted
Rt. 1 Box 71
Williams AZ 86046

Peace of Mind
5835 East 34th Street
Tucson AZ 85711

Search Triad, Inc.
P.O. Box 1432
Litchfield AZ 85340

CALIFORNIA

Judy Alboert, M.A.
17610 Beach Blvd. 38
Huntington Beach CA 92647

Gayle L. Beckstead
2180 Clover St.
Simi Valley CA 93065

Martin Brandfon, Attorney
P.O. Box 1923
Burlingame CA 94010

Jean Gold, LCSW
4950 Barrance Pkwy 308
Irvine CA 92714

Patsy Hankins, MSW, LCSW
930 Enterprise St.
Inglewood CA 90302

Mary Lou Kozub
2027 Finch Court
Simi Valley CA 90302

Carol Longoria
P.O. Box 24095
San Jose CA 95154

Nancy O'Neill
1430 Henry St.
Berkeley CA 94709

Barbara Mae Specht
4501 Riverside Ave, Sp. 47
Anderson CA 96007

Dean Watt
5855 Naples Plaza 306
Long Beach CA 90803

Loyd D. White
30130 town Center Dr.
Laguna Niguel CA 92677

Ms. J. Leslie Witham
19120 Nordhoff St. Sp. 3
Northridge CA 91324

Dorothy Yturriaga
P.O. Box 24095
San Jose CA 95154

Alberta F. Sorenson
P.O. Box 3000
Camarillo CA 93010

May Boyden
36 Christamon West
Irvine CA 92714

Elizabeth Oliveira
P.O. Box 1067
Highland CA 92346

Delayn Curtis
4784 Horseshoe Lane
Riverside CA 92509

Adoptee Identity Discovery
   AID
Box 2159
Sunnyvale CA 94087

Adoptees Liberty Movement
   Assn. ALMA-Western
   Reg. Office
Box 9333
North Hollywood Ca 91609

Adoptees Liberty Movement
   Assn. ALMA Chapter
Box 2341
Alameda CA 94501

Adoptees Liberty Movement
   Assn. ALMA Chapter
Box 271
Vina CA 96092

Adoptees Liberty Movement
   Assn. ALMA Chapter
Box 8081
Sacramento CA 95818

Adoptees Movement
Rt. 2, Box 2654-Z
Red Bluffs CA 96080

Adoptees Research Association
Box 304
Montrose CA 91020

Adoptees', Birthparents'
   Association ABA
P.O. Box 33
Camarillo CA 93011

Adoption Reality
2180 Clover Street
Simi Valley CA 93065

Birth Family Research
2027 Finch Court
Simi Valley CA 93063

Central Coast Adoption
   Support Grp.
Box 5165
Santa Maria CA 93456

Concerned United
   Birthparents CUB
   Rep. Delayn Curtis
4784 Horseshoe Lane
Riverside CA 92509

Concerned United
   Birthparents CUB Branch
9538 Tweedy Lane
Downey CA 90240

Concerned United
   Birthparents CUB Branch
11514 Ventura Bl. A179
Studio City CA 91604

Concerned United
   Birthparents CUB
   Rep. Joan P. Grabe
8632 Coolwoods Dr.
Sacramento CA 95825

Concerned United
   Birthparents CUB
   Rep. Linda Kane
235 W. Quinto 2
Santa Barbara CA 93105

Concerned United
   Birthparents CUB
   Rep. Mary Medlin
P.O. Box 171302
San Diego CA 92117

Concerned United
   Birthparents CUB
   Rep. Sara Crystal
467 42nd. St.
Oakland CA 94609

Independent Search
   Consultants ISC
Box 10192
Costa Mesa CA 92627

Los angelos Co. Adoption
   Search Assn. La Casa
11514 Ventura Blvd. A-179
Studio City CA 91604

Organized Adoption Search
   Information
   Service-OASIS
P.O. Box 375
Mc Cloud CA 96057

Parenting Resources
1633 E. 4th. St. Suite 288
Santa Ana CA 92701

Post Adoption Center for Ed. &
   Research - PACER
477 15th St. Rm 200
Oakland CA 94612

Professional Adoption Search
   Team PAST
Box 24095
San Jose CA 95154

Reaching Out
Box 42749
Los Angelos CA 90042

Search and Find
P.O. Box 8765
Riverside CA 92515

Search Finders of California
P.O. Box 24595
San Jose CA 95154

Tennessee Adoptees in Search
4598 Rosewood
Montclair CA 91763

TRIAD Research
300 Golden West
Shafter CA 93263

United Adoptees and Parents
   of Central Calif.
9303 E. Bullard
Clovis CA 93612

COLORADO

Adoptees on Search
Contact Stn.27 Box 323
Lakewood CO 80212

Concerned United
   Birthparents CUB Branch
Box 22904
Denver CO 80222

Orphan Voyage
   Headquarters O.V.
2141 Road 2300
Cedaredge CO 81413

CONNECTICUT

Adoptees Liberty Movement
   Assn. ALMA Chapter
55 Woods Grove Rd.
Huntington CT 06484

Ties that Bind
P.O. Box 3119
Milford CT 06460

Adoptees Search Connection
1203 Hill St.
Suffield CT 06078

Concerned United
   Birthparents CUB Branch
Box 526
Rocky Hill CT 06382

WASHINGTON

Marilyn Moore
L'Enfant Plaza Box 23674
Washington DC 20024

American Adoption Congress
AAC, Inc.
L'Enfant Plaza Box 44040
Washington DC 20026

Concerned United
Birthparents CUB Branch
Box 23641 L'Enfant Plaza
Washington DC 20024

Investigative Research
Services
L'Enfant Plaza Box 23674
Washington DC 20024

Kinship, Inc.
232 2nd St. SE
Washington DC 20003

DELAWARE

Deleware Tri-Love
Box 526
New Castle DE 19720

Solomon;s Child/Trialog
Children's Bureau of DE
2005 Baynard Blvd.
Wilmington DE 19711

FLORIDA

Charles Eckert
2425 Brengle Ave 28
Orlando FL 32808

Geortia D. Humphrey
1022 Everglade Dr.
Niceville FL 32578

Deby Raiford
1501 Girvin Rd.
Jacksonville FL 32225

Adoptees Liberty Movement
Assn. ALMA Chapter
Box 4358
Lauderdale FL 33338

Adoption Consultants, Inc.
9320 S.W. 170th St.
Miami FL 33157

Adoption Triangle Ministries,
Inc. ATM
Box 1860
Cape Coral FL 33910

Concerned United
Birthparents CUB
Rep. Brenda Rodriquez
455 Branan Field Rd.
Middleburg FL 32068

Organized Adp'n Search Info.
Service OASIS Chapter
P.O. Box 31612
St. Petersburg FL 33732

Organized Adp'n Search Info.
Service
OASIS-Headquaters
P.O. Box 53-0761
Miami Shores FL 33153

Organized Adp'n Search Info.
Service OASIS Chapter
Box 11
Valrico FL 33594

Organized Adp'n Search Info.
Service OASIS Chapter
Box 3874
Sarasota FL 33578

Orphan Voyage Chapter
13505 SW 100 CT
Miami FL 33176

Orphan Voyage Chapter
12094 Old Country RD.
West Palm Beach FL 33411

Orphan Voyage Chapter
P.O. Box 312
Oklawaha FL 32679

Orphan Voyage Chapter
1130 NE 92nd St.
Miami Shores FL 33138

Orphan Voyage Chapter
3906 Pepperill Dr.
Tampa FL 33624

Orphan Voyage of Florida
Box 10909
Jacksonville FL 32247

GEORGIA

Adoptee's Search Network
3317 Spring Creek Drive
Conyers GA 30208

Adoptees Liberty Movement
Assn. ALMA Chapter
62 Park Gate Dr.
Atlanta GA 30328

Caring Heart
P.O. Box 361111
Decatur GA 30032

Concerned United
Birthparents CUB
Rep. Joann Howard
3374 Aztewc Rd. Apt. 35C
Doraville GA 30340

Roots and Wings
Box 32
Tucker GA 30084

HAWAII

Adoptees Liberty Movement
Assn. ALMA Chapter
58-250C Kam Hwy.
Haleieva HI 96712

IOWA

Adoptees Quest
408 Buresh
Iowa City IA 52240

Adoptive Experience Group
1105 Freemont
Des Moines IA 50316

Concerned United
Birthparents CUB Branch
Box 8294
Cedar Rapids IA 52408

Concerned United
Birthparents CUB Branch
500 Kimberly Lane
Des Moines IA 50317

Iowa Reference & Reunion
Library
P.O. Box 9191
Cedar Rapids IA 52409

Orphan Voyage Chapter
Box 21
Cedar IA 52543

IDAHO

Adoptees Liberty Movement
Assn. ALMA Chapter
Box 4281
Boise ID 83704

ILLINOIS

Adoptees Liberty Movement
Assn. ALMA Chapter
Box 74
Lebannon IL 62254

Adoptees Liberty Movement
Assn. ALMA Chapter
Box 81
Bloomington IL 61701

Adoptees Liberty Movement
Assn. ALMA Chapter
P.O. Box 59345
Chicago IL 60659

Concerned United
Birthparents
156 W. Burton Place
Chicago IL 60610

Hidden Birthright
Box 1651
Springfield IL 62705

Protect the Children Inc.
P.O. Box 49
Steger IL 60475

Search Research
Box 48
Chicago Ridge IL 60415

Tracers, LTD.
Gari-Sue Greene
P.O. Box 205
Round Lake Beach
IL 60073

Truth Seekers in Adoption
Box 366
Prospect Heights IL 60070

Yesterday's Children, Inc.
Box 1554
Evanston IL 60204

INDIANA

Mickey Carty
P.O. Box 1062
Richmond IN 47374

Martha Barrow
Box 441
New Haven IN 46774

Adoptee's Identity
Doorway AID
P.O. Box 361
South Bend IN 46637

Adoptees Family Circle
AFC
P.O. Box 1062
Richmond IN 47374

Adoptees Liberty
Movement Assn.
ALMA-Indianapolis Group
Box 207
Chalmers IN 47929

Concerned United
Birthparents CUB
Rep. Karen Bolen
4501 Farnsworth
Indianapolis IN 46241

Reunion Registry of Indiana
Box 361
South Bend In 46624

Search Committee-Madison
County Historical Society
2514 E. 6th St.
Anderson IN 46012

Search for Tomorrow, Inc.
P.O. Box 441
New Haven IN 46774

Seek
213 Dreamwold Ms
Michigan City IN 46360

Support of Search SOS
P.O. Box 1292
Kokomo IN 46901

KANSAS

Susan R. Lovett
5402 Polo
Wichita KS 67208

Adoptees Liberty Movement
Assn. ALMA Chapter
Box 532
Leavenworth KS 66048

Wichita Adult Adoptees
5402 Polo
Wichita KS 67208

KENTUCKY

Adoptees Looking
in Kentucky, Inc. ALINK
P.O. Box 866
Lexington KY 40587

Concerned United
Birthparents CUB
Rep. Susan Secchi
2159 Lansil Rd.
Lexington KY 40504

LOUISIANA

Adoptees Birthrights
Committee Headquarters
ABC
Cox 7213
Metairie LA 70010

Adoption Triad Network Lake
Charles Chapter
Box 6175
Lake Charles LA 70606

Adoption Triad Network
Baton Rouge Chapter
511 Blue Bell
Port Allen LA 70605

Adoption Triad Network
Monroe Chapter
P.O. Box 324
Swartz LA 71281

Adoption Triad Network
Morgan City Chapter
Box 1140
Morgan City LA 70381

Adoption Triad Network, Inc.
Headquarters - ATN
P.O. Box 3932
Lafayette LA 70502

MASSACHUSETTS

Adoptees Liberty Movement
Assn. ALMA Champter
P.O. Box 595
North Andover MA 01845

The Adoption Connection, Inc.
TAC
11 Peabody Square, Rm. 6
Peabody MA 01960

Cape Cod Association for Truth
in Adoption - CCATA
Box 606
Woods Hole MA 02543

Concerned United
Birthparents CUB Branch
Harvard Square Box 396
Cambridge MA 02238

MARYLAND

Adoptees in Search
Box 41016
Bethesda MD 20014

Adoptees Search Organization
Inc. ASO
P.O. Box 55198
Ft. Washington MD 20744

Adoption Connection
Exchange ACE
P.O. Box 2724
Laurel MD 20708

MAINE

Lois Thurston
Rfd 4 Box 14
Gardiner ME 04345

Adoption Search Consultants
of ME. ASC ME
P.O. Box 2793
South Portland ME 04106

Concerned United
Birthparents CUB
Rep. Carol Simpson
Rfd 2 Hiltons Lane
No. Berwick ME 03906

Orphan Voyage Chapter
10 Meadow Way
South Portland ME 04106

MICHIGAN

Chris Spurr
1602 Cole
Birmingham MI 48008

Adoptee's Search for
Knowledge Inc. ASK
P.O. Box 762
E. Lansing MI 48823

Adoptees Liberty Movement
Assn. ALMA Chapter
4082 Harbor Point Dr.
Muskegon MI 49441

Adoption Communication
Triangle ACT
32715 Dorsey
Westland MI 48185

Adoption Identity Movement of
Michigan - AIM
P.O. Box 20092
Detroit MI 48220

Adoption Identity Movement
AIM
P.O. Box 9265
Grand Rapids MI 49509

Adoption Insight
P.O. Box 153
Otsego MI 49078

Concerned United
Birthparents CUB
Rep. Kathy Webb
801 Granger Ave.
Ann Arbor MI 48104

Concerned United
Birthparents CUB
Rep. Deanna Rogers
8107 Webster Rd.
Mt. Morris MI 48458

Mid-Michigan Adoption
Identity Movement - AIM
13636 Podunk Rd.
Cedar Springs MI 49319

Re-Traced Roots
P.O. Box 1390
Muskegon MI 49442

Roots and Reunions
P.O. Box 121
L'Anse MI 49946

Truths in the Adoption Triad
8107 Webster Rd.
Mt. Morris MI 48458

Quebec Quest Reunion
Registry
Box 463
Uion MI 49130

MINNESOTA

Adoptees Liberty Movement
Assn. ALMA Chapter
7048 Progress Rd.
Hugo MN 55038

Concerned United
Birthparents CUB Branch
9450 Wellington Lane
Ninneapolis MN 55369

Liberal Education for Adoptive
Families - LEAF
23247 Lofton Court No.
Scania MN 55073

Minnesota Reunion Registry
23247 Lofton Ct. No.
Scandia MN 55073

MISSOURI

Adoptees Liberty Movement
Assn. ALMA Chapter
P.O. Box 50122
Clayton MO 63105

Christian Family Services, Inc.
8812 Manchester Blvd.
St. Louis MO 63144

Concerned United
Birthparents CUB
Rep. Susan Foglesong
7000 Jackson
Kansas City MO 64132

Kansas City Adult Adoptees
organization
Box 15225
Kansas City MO 64106

Searchline
P.O. Box 274
Lampe MO 65681

Southwestern Missouri Adult
Adoptees
Rt. 5, Box 172
Joplin MO 64801

Southwestern Missouri Adult
Adoptees
3138 Kisimee Court
Springfield MO 65806

MISSISSIPPI

Adoptees Liberty Movement
Assn. ALMA Chapter
Box 212
Columbus MS 39701

NORTH CAROLINA

Adoptees Liberty Movement
Assn. ALMA Chapter
Box 901
Madison NC 27025

Adoptees Together
Box 16532
Greensboro NC 27406

Adoption Information
Exchange AIE
800-54 Whitesides Rd.
Gastonia NC 28052

Adoption Information
Exchange AIE
P.O. Box 4153
Chapel Hill NC 27514

Concerned United
Birthparents CUB Branch
4916 Brentwood Drive
Durham NC 27713

NEBRASKA

Adoptees Liberty Movement
Assn. ALMA Chapter
Box 202
Fairfield NE 68938

Midwest Adoption Triad
Box 37262
Omaha NE 68137

NEW HAMPSHIRE

Concerned United
Birthparents CUB
Headquarters
595 Central Ave.
Dover NH 03820

Concerned United
Birthparents CUB
Rep. Susan Daggett
Box 64
Merrimack NH 03054

NEW JERSEY

Adoptive Liberty Movement
Assn. ALMA Chapter
Box 627-M
Morristown NJ 07960

Adoptive Parents for Open
Records
9 Marjoie Dr.
Hackettstown NJ 07840

Birthdates
117 Nelson Ave.
Jersey City NJ 07307

Origins
Box 105
Oakhurst NJ 07755

NEW MEXICO

Leonie D. Boehmer
805 Alvarado NE
Albuquerque NM 87108

Operation Identity, Inc.
13101 Blackstone NE
Albuquerque NM 87111

NEVADA

Martha L. Reinhart
4478 Casa Blanca
Las Vegas NV 89121

Heritage, Incorporated
P.O. Box 85424
Las Vegas NV 89185

International Soundex
Reunion Registry - ISRR
P.O. Box 2312
Carson City NV 89702

NEW YORK

Dennis McCarthy
42 Morris St.
Auborn NY 13021

Resalie Schwab
3 Town House Circle
Great Neck NY 11021

Adoptees Information Service
AIS
19 Marion Ave.
Mt. Vernon NY 10552

Adoptees Liberty Movement
Assn. ALMA Chapter
Box 806
Bolton Landing NY 12814

Adoptees Liberty Movement
Assn. ALMA Chapter
Box 10441
Rochester NY 14610

Adoptees Liberty Movement
Assn. ALMA Headquaters
Box 154 Wash. Bridge Stn.
New York City NY 10033

Adoptees Liberty Movement
Assn. ALMA Chapter
Box 809
Beacon NY 12508

The Adoption Circle
3 Town House Circle 2A
Great Neck NY 11021

Adoption Friendship Circle
P.O. Box 7067
Endicott NY 13760

Adoption Task Force
P.O. Box 1576
Southhampton NY 11968

Always in Me AIM
Box 454
Orchard Park NY 14126

Birthparent Support Network
P.O. Box 120
North White Plains NY 10603

Concerned United
  Birthparents CUB Branch
2 Stemmer Lane
Suffern NY 10901

Concerned United
  Birthparents CUB
  Rep. Susan Fuller
102 North St.
Manlius NY 13104

Far Horizons
Box 621
Cortland NY 13045

National Adoptive Search
  Registry NASR, Inc.
P.O. Box 2051
Great Neck NY 11022

Suffolk Adoption Search &
  Support SASS
10 Janice Lane
Selden NY 11784

The Right To Know
P.O. Box 52
Old Westbury NY 11568

OHIO

John W. Weiss
4309 Hamilton Av. 22
Cincinnati OH 45223

Laurie Herr
1195 Hillbrook
Lnacaster OH 43103

Adoptees Search Rights Assn.
  ASRA
Box 8713
Toledo OH 43623

Adoptees Search Rights Assn.
  ASRA
Box 2249
Cleveland OH 44102

Chosen Children
311 Springbrook
Dayton OH 45405

Concerned United
  Birthparents CUB Branch
Wausen OH 43567

Concerned United
  Birthparents CUB
  Rep. Carol Hunter
5248 York Rd. SW
Rataskala OH 43062

Lost & Found Search &
  Support Group
P.O. Box 1033
Cuyahoga Falls OH 44223

Reunite, Inc.
P.O. Box 694
Reynoldsburg OH 43068

Sunshine
1175 Virginia Ave.
Akron OH 44306

OKLAHOMA

Lynda Lu Reed
8220 N.W. 114th
Oklahoma City OK 73132

Adoptees as Adults
8220 N.W. 114th St.
Oklahoma City OK 73132

Willows Graduates
RR 8, Box 324
Claremore OK 74017

OREGON

Mrs. Kathy Brown
1076 Queens Branch Rd.
Rogue River OR 97537

Nancie J. Finley
5256 S.W. Nebraska
Portland OR 97219

Helen Gallagher
4001 Potter 73
Eugene OR 97405

Jeanne Macomber
953 N.E. 10th St.
Grants Pass OR 97526

Birthparents in Oregon BIO
P.O. Box 17521
Portland OR 97405

Family Ties
4001 Potter 73
Eugene OR 97405

Oregon Adoptive Rights
  Association OARA
Box 1332
Beaverton OR 97520

Southern Oregon Adoptive
  Rights
492 Willow
Ashland OR 97520

PENNSYLVANIA

Adoption Forum, Inc.
6808 Ridge Ave.
Philadelphia PA 19128

Adoption Lifeline ALA
914 28th Ave.
Altoona PA 15214

Concerned United
  Birthparents CUB Branch
Box 7673
Pittsburgh PA 15214

Concerned United
  Birthparents CUB
  Rep. Alicia Giesa
Box 1156
Bryn Mawr PA 19010

Concerned United
  Birthparents CUB
  Rep. Chris Frank
2800 W. Chestnut Ave.
Altoona PA 16603

P.A.S.T.
3847 Admidon Ave.
Erie PA 16510

Pittsburg Adoption Lifeline
  PAL
P.O. Box 52
Gibsonia PA 15044

RHODE ISLAND

Parents & Adoptees Liberty
  Movement - PALM
861 Michell's Lane
Middletown RI 02840

Search, LTD.
Rfd. 1, Box 337
Ashaway RI 02804

SOUTH CAROLINA

Adoptees & Birthparents
  in Search
Box 551
Cayce West Columbia
SC 29171

Adoptees & Birthparents
  in Search
Box 6426B
Greenville SC 29606

Triad, Inc.
Box 4778
Culumbia SC 29240

SOUTH DAKOTA

Adoptees Liberty Movement
  Assn. ALMA Chapter
1325 S. Bahnson
Sioux Falls SD 57103

TENNESSEE

Adoptees Liberty Movement
  Assn. ALMA Chapter
Box 15064
Chattanooga TN 37415

Adult Adoptees and Birth
  Parents in Search
Box 3572
Chattanooga TN 37404

Concerned United
  Birthparents CUB
  Rep. Norma F. Samsel
2601 Holston, Lakemore
Morristown TN 37814

Independent Search &
  Adoption Consultants
6536 Ferncrest
Memphis TN 38134

Rights Of Origin Tennesseans
  in Search - ROOTS
P.O. Box 11522

Tennessee Adoptees in Search
P.O. Box 8684
Chattanooga TN 37411

Tennessee The Right to Know
Box 34344
Memphis TN 38134

TEXAS

Adoptees Liberty Movement
  Assn. ALMA Chapter
Box 5735
Austin TX 78763

Adoption Awareness Center
  AAC
615 Elm at McCullough
San Antonio TX 78213

Adoption Counseling and
  Consultation
1550 NE Loop 410 S134
San Antonio TX 78209

Concerned United
  Birthparents CUB
  Branch-Dallas Area
Box 1527
Plano TX 75074

The Right to Know
Box 1409
Grand Prairie TX 75051

Search Finders of Texas
150 Terrell Plaza 49
San Antonio TX 78208

Searchline of Texas Chapter
Box 4101
Amarillo TX 79116

Searchline of Texas, Inc.
725 Burnwood
Irving TX 75062

Triangle Search
5730 Crestgrove
Corpus Christi TX 78415

UTAH

Bonnie P. Coxey
P.O. Box 41
Hooper UT 84315

Carolyn Jones
P.O. Box 8124
Salt Lake City UT 84108

Adoptees Liberty Movement
  Assn. ALMA Chapter
Box 11383
Salt Lake City UT 84147

Concerned United
  Birthparents CUB Branch
Box 1613
Sandy UT 84091

Interstate Genealogists
369 E. 900 South
Salt Lake City UT 84111

VIRGINIA

Adoptee & Natural Parents
  Inc. ANPO
37 West Pollux Circle
Portsmouth VA 23701

Parents & Adoptees Together
1500 Fort Hill Dr.
Richmond VA 23226

VERMONT

Concerned United
  Birthparents CUB
  Rep. Carol Gile
Rd 1 Box 716
Bridgeport VT 05734

WASHINGTON

Washington Adoptees Rights
  Movement WARM
220 Kirkland Ave 10
Kirkland WA 98033

WISCONSIN

Ginny Whitehouse
3102 Lakeland Ave.
Madison WI 53704

Mary Ann Neibuhr
4221 Tomscott Trail
Madison WI 53704

Elton Smith
6706 Revere Ave.
Milwaukee WI 53213

Adoption Information &
  Direction AID
P.O. Box 3397
Madison WI 53704

Adoption Information &
  Direction AID
P.O. Box 2152
Appleton WI 54913

Adoption Information &
  Direction AID
Box 662
Oshkosh WI 54902

Adoption Information &
  Direction AID
Box 111
Cudahy WI 53110

Adoption Information &
  Direction AID
4511 Woodridge Dr.
Eau Claire WI 54701

WEST VIRGINIA

Society's Tri-Angle, LTD.
411 Cabell Court
Huntington WV 25703

The Lost Children
312 8th Ave.
St. Albans WV 25177

WYOMING

Adoptees Liberty Movement
  Assn. ALMA Chapter
123 E. Parks
Riverton WY 82501

CANADA

Adoption Research Project
3231 Williams Rd.
Richmond B.C. V7E 1H8
Canada

Birthparent and Relative
  Group of Canada, Inc.
5317 145 Avenue
Edmonton Alberta T5A 4E9
Canada

Canadian Adoptees Reform
  Association of B.C.
202-4381 Fraser St.
Vancouver B.C. V5V 4G4
Canada

Parent Finders Chapter
Box 214 Station G
Calgary Alberta T3A 2G2
Canada

Parent Finders Chapter
Box 12031
Edmonton Alberta T5J 3L2
Canada

Parent Finders Chapter
Box 1991
Hope B.C. VOX 1LO Canada

Parent Finders Chapter
Box 84 Main Postal Stn.
Kamloops B.C. V2C 5K3
Canada

Parent Finders Chapter
1062 Maple Close
Quesnell B.C. V2J 3W3
Canada

Parent Finders Chapter
134 Brigade Drive
Prince George B.C. V2M 4N6
Canada

Parent Finders National Office
1408 W. 45th Ave.
Vancover B.C. V6M 2H1
Canada

Parent Finders Chapter
3023 Volmer Road
Victoria B.C. V9B 2H5 Canada

Parent Finders Chapter
28 Laurel Leaf Lane
Winnipeg Manitobe R2P 1S1
Canada

Parent Finders Chapter
Box 263
Rothsay N.B. E0G 2W0
Canada

Parent Finders Chapter
P.O. Box 363
Bedford Nova Scotia B4A 2X3
Canada

Parent Finders Chapter
Box 5211 Postal Station F
Ottawa Ontario K2C 3H5
Canada

Parent Finders Chapter
1256 Winter Ave.
Oshawa Ontario L1H 1T5
Canada

Parent Finders Chaptr
  (Newfoundland)
7 Welland St. South
Thorold Ontario L2V 2B3
Canada

Parent Finders Chapter
146 Richmond
Thorold Ontario L2V 3H4
Canada

Parent Finders Chapter
36 Woodbridge Rd.
Hamilton Ontario L8K 3C9
Canada

Parent Finders Incorporated
53 Sheppard Ave. W.
Toronto Ontario M2N 1M4
Canada

Parent Finders Chapter
Box 16
Rutheven Ontario N0P 2G0
Canada

Parent Finders Chapter
521 Oak Park Drive
London Ontario N6H 3N6
Canada

Parent Finders Chapter
161 Victoria Ave.
Point Edward Ontario
N7V 1H4 Canada

Parent Finders Chapter
110 Turnbull Ave.
Wallaceburg Ontario
N8A 3M7 Canada

Parent Finders Chapter
617 Camelot Dr.
Subbury ontario P3B 2M9
Canada

Parent Finders Chapter
63 Meadow Park Cresent
Sault St. Marie Ontario
P6A 4H1 Canada

Parent Finders Chapter
P.O. Box 932
Delson Quebec J0L 1G0
Canada

Parent Finders Chapter
Box 244
Morse Saskatchewan S0H 3C0
Canada

FOREIGN COUNTRIES

Adoption Information Services
  - Jigsaw
CGPO Box 5260 BB
Melbourne 3001 Australia

Adoption Jigsaw W.A., Inc.
Post Office Box 252
Hillary's 6025 Australia

9.0 SKIP TRACING FOR PROFIT

Skip tracing for profit is a big business. In fact, it is the only thing some individuals in the field do. Fees for such services vary depending on the purpose of the trace and the amount of information initially provided.

Some outfits charge a flat rate as low as $25.00 to $65.00 per hour plus expenses. At those prices the bucks add up fast and so does the profit.

Missing Witnesses and Process Serving

A process server is someone who serves (delivers) subpoenas, complaints, eviction notices, or any other type of legal document. Most states require process servers to be licensed and bonded. However, few require a test or any preparation for licensing except a clean criminal record and licensing fee of somewhere around $100.00.

Private process servers make good money. They usually get the "paper" someone else could not serve because of their inability to locate the subject. They charge by the hour, and if they're good, are kept very busy.

Attorneys often need to locate missing witnesses. In many cases, by the time the case goes to court, years have passed and many of the witnesses can no longer be found. The difficulty with these assignments is that they are usually rush in nature and difficult to collect on if you are unsuccessful. Attorneys do not like to pay as it is; try to get their cooperation when you cannot find their key witness!

Missing Heirs

This type of business can be very profitable. It is usually worked one of two ways:

With the first method, the deceased normally has a last will and testament. In order to settle the estate, the executor (usually an attorney) hires someone to locate all the living heirs. In this process, he hires an investigator specializing in this field and pays him/her a flat or hourly rate.

In the second method, the deceased does not have a last will and testament and the estate goes into probate. If no claims are made the entire estate goes to the state and its proceeds are dumped into the General Fund.

Investigators working the second method hang around probate court and wait for an uncontested filing to be made. They then examine the case and determine the dollar amount involved. If the estate is of any size (say greater than $50,000) they then throw together a contract and try to locate any heirs. When one is found the contract is consummated and the investigator is paid a "finder's fee" at a percentage (30-50%) agreed upon in the contract.

This is hard work and often unrewarding. Good outfits consider two or three settlements a year to be good business. But then again, 50% of $1,000,000 is not bad!

Credit And Loan Skips

Anybody in the credit business has a collection problem. Probably anybody in any business has a collection problem. To actually collect the debts, most states require licenses. But no state requires a license to locate the debtors as long as you are an agent of the creditor. Quite simply, if they say "go find them," you are their agent. Banks, credit companies, loan outfits, utility companies, retail and service companies all need help in locating dead beats. Even collection companies use outside help in locating skips.

Depending on the arrangements, clients are willing to pay up to 50% of the amount owed to find the people and collect. Even on a flat fee, this type of work is profitable.

With the advent of credit cards, this form of business has boomed. It is not uncommon for a small town bank to have *several thousand* bad accounts! Larger ones often have hundreds or thousands of dollars written off or about to be. Working these cases under any agreement can be profitable. An experienced skip tracer can work as many as 50 at a time. Finding only two a day can make a fine day's pay.

Missing Stockholders

Uncashed dividend checks are a problem. Federal law requires corporations possessing them to keep detailed records, then eventually give the money to the appropriate party when found. For a large corporation, this is very costly. Often just the postage involved far exceeds the dividend. These companies are willing to pay you to locate these people. The standard rate is usually somewhere between $3.00 and $5.00 per name. At that rate, you better be good or very lucky.

Missing Insurance Claimants and Policy Holders

Like any business, insurance companies need to keep track of their customers. Believe it or not even claimants (the ones receiving payment from the insurance company) disappear. As a matter of practice insurance companies like to keep tabs on the people they pay off. Generally, this requires outside help.

They are also constantly looking for witnesses, family members, friends, neighbors and such when defending a claim. They also become very interested when someone with a life insurance policy disappears. By law, after several years, even without finding a body, they mast pay off the survivors. When an insured disappears, they act fast and usually are very willing to pay for good help.

Missing Alumni and Association Members

Big associations do not like to loose track of their members (it can mean loosing a great deal of money during fund raisers!). "Inactive lists" are usually available from associations for the asking, and if worked properly, can be money makers. Postal searches (by mail) and telephone directory assistance are usually the only steps taken, as the rate runs no more than $2.00 or $3.00 for each successful locate.

Adoptees Seeking Natural Parents

This is a full time job. More than ever before people are desiring to know who they really are. Most states consider both the adoptee and birth parents as protected groups.

For those in this end of the business, there is more business than can be handled. Rates vary, but expect to charge around $35.00 per hour, plus expenses.

Missing And Runaway Spouses

For whatever reason, this line of work is booming. Spouses walk out on one another every day, and though the reasons vary the effect is still the same. Hearts are broken and bills are left unpaid.

This is my favorite line of work and for a good reason. It is easy and very profitable. The trail is generally very fresh and clean. The skip is unexperienced and plagued with old habits. Most cases take only several days to solve.

Rates are usually hourly, running about $40.00 per hour plus expenses.

General Practice

Most investigation outfits will locate missing persons as a service, although some specialize in it. In either case, if run properly it can be profitable. Rates run between $30.00 and $65.00 per hour plus expenses. If you choose this line, be sure to check and see what licenses are required before you start. For those toying with the idea, test a simple classified advertisement. Depending on the response, you should be able to reasonably estimate local demand for your services.

Missing Persons Located
(Your telephone number)

or

We Find Anyone!
(Your telelphone number)

Generally, this approach has limited success. If you want to advertise use the yellow pages. They are expensive but they sure do work. I recommend at least a one-inch display for starters.

10.0 HOW IT WORKS: A PRACTICAL EXAMPLE

Let me now walk you through a "typical" locate. From a practical standpoint, let us assume we at least know the following information about our subject:

Full Name (including middle initial)
Last Known Address (2 years old)

Step 1:   I would immediately call directory assistance and run the name in every city within fifty miles of the last known address. I would then call every listing under that name and ask them if they ever lived at the last known address. I would be sure to tell them I was not looking for them but "Mr. (So and So) the guy who used to live next door...because he just inherited a shopping center on the East Coast."

I would be sure to follow up on every lead and not miss a trick.

Step 2:   I would then call or go (if practical) to the district post office and run a postal search on the last known address and on the ones on either side and to the back of it (if I could determine them).

If our subject moved without a change of address, so be it. But I would check the neighbors as well. Say for example we find two of the three neighbors moved with no forwarding address, and the remaining neighbor has been living there for twenty-five years.

Step 3:   I would "cross-street" the neighbor who has been there for twenty-five years and call them. After fifteen minutes of conversation with them, this is what I would have discovered:

A.   The house in question (the one our subject used to live in) is owned by a Mr. Arjay Miller, and his telephone number is (213) 123-4567. He has owned this house for the past fifteen years and rents it out; still does.

B.   Our subject had actually two names (the neighbors often got their mail by mistake).

C.   He was married to a woman named "Sue," and she had two children, by a previous marriage.

D.   Sue went to school at night, and was a beautician during the day. "Worked right up the street..at Sal's."

E.   "Cute kids, too. Susan was about seven and Carl was about nine, I think."

F.   "Now Sammie, he was another story...I don't think he ever worked. He was a healthy looking guy, too." (Description provided.) "But he got hurt real bad on the job, or so he said."

G.   "I don't think they ever paid their bills, either. There are still bill collectors looking for them. Say, are you one of them?"

Now in this short senario, I have provided you no less than fifteen clues. Make a list of your own and compare it to mine:

1.   Mr. Miller probably still has the original rental agreement signed and completed by my subject for the rental of the house. Subject probably owes his money, too, so Mr. Miller will likely cooperate. Miller may also know the name of their bank because their last rent check bounced.

2.   Current resident may still get mail addressed to the subject. If any are lenders they are often able to provide clues.

3.   Two new names. Back to the telephone directory and post office (run "Sue's" name too).

4.   Probably recently married, as the neighbor had mentioned the children were from a previous marriage.

5.   One child is in school, and may still be in school, or the school knows where they might have moved to.

6.   Wife also went to school (night).

7.   Wife was a beautician and probably was licensed by the city or state.

8.   Check out the wife's ex-employer, Sal's.

9.   Talk to employees at Sal's. Sue my have left some friends behind. You may have to run postal searches on key employees if they have since left.

10.   Husband probably was injured on the job. He may have filed with Workman's Compensation or a civil suit against his former employer.

11.   Contact local credit bureaus and see where the subject stands with them.

12.   Check small claims and municipal court for non-payment of rent or collection lawsuits.

13.   Check criminal records and determine if unpaid bills and debts caused problems.

14.   Check all city and state licensing agencies and see if family had a business or any member had any special skills.

15.   Check voters registration under all names including the wife.

I would also immediately do a statewide DMV search, for both vehicles and accidents. Do not leave a rock unturned and follow up on all leads.

You should by now see how easy it really is. What used to seem like worthless information is now priceless. More than likely that special someone who you are looking for is only a telephone call away.

11.0 SOME OTHER HELPFUL HINTS

Business Cards and Stationery

Review again the fourth chapter which discusses the use of business cards and stationery. As a "professional" in the field of investigation, these tools are invaluable. Read on for some extra hints.

While in the field I probably give out at least twenty-five business cards a day. As a general rule I give one out to every person I meet. A business card is almost considered a license. Being such, take advantge of it. I rarely hesitate to tell anyone what I do or what my business is. Not only does it generate new business, but it makes people relaxed to know who you are and what your line of work is.

In many cases, unless you are "one of them," people will not cooperate with you. Insurance companies are very much that way. When dealing with these companies, be an agent, a claims representative or an underwriter. Just make sure you know the language, and are able to stay calm.

NEVER impersonate a police officer or another government official. This practice is frowned upon and not taken lightly. However, I often identify myself as an investigator and usually get high quality cooperation. Try it when you feel comfortable.

As for stationery, I have a ton of it, and use it every day. A letter typed on a letterhead turns heads. With the use of a copy machine AND a good quality typewriter, you can turn anyone's letterhead into your own. Just think of all the things you could do with a selection of thirty or so business letterheads!

Another must is a post office box. Either a private box or a regular post office box will do. A P.O. box will prevent other people (who haven't read this book!) from finding you. Additionally, by using a single box you can create an infinite number of new addresses for yourself. For example, to the box number add suite number (anything) or draw number (anything). If it is a business box, use: "attention: (Your Name)" or any name you wish to use.

A post office box also prevents visitors from knocking on your door. "Lookie-lou's" cannot check you out or your operation.

Another big help is the telephone answering machine. I hate to use them, but in this business they are a must. They are easy to use and quite acceptable. One saved call could pay for a hundred machines.

11.1 START A FILE

Regardless of who you are searching for, or for what reason, the first step is to start a file on the subject. These files are called "case files." In the case file you will keep letters, photographs, day-to-day reports, and any piece of information that you may attain concerning your subject. Assign each subject a case number. Then file the cases by case number, not by subject's last name. For the assignment of a case number, I use a procedure somewhat like this:

Say for example, today's date was June 5, 1985, the case number might be 06-23585; 06 for the month of June, 235 for the two hundreth and thirty-fifth case of the year, and 85 for the year. For filing purposes, we are not necessarily interested in the exact day we obtained the case. Our log books are the reason why.

You will need two log books (any form of bound paper will do). In the first book you will list chronologically the case number, subject's name, date investigation began, and the date the investigation was completed.

Case Number	Subject's Name	Date Opened	Date Closed
06-23585	John Doe	5 June 1981	12 June 1981

In the second log book, you will list by case number and date all of your day-to-day activities while actively investigating. (Be sure to record your expenses and your mileage!) The records may be used for tax purposes but more importantly, they allow you to operate more efficiently and professionally. One more system I recommend is to start a 3 x 5 card file of all your subjects in alphabetical order. Included on the card should be the case number and whatever else you might think important. This system allows you to index a subject by name, case number, or date. Convenient, effective and professional. For those of you who wish to not get this carried away, I still insist at the very least, a case file be made. It is the only reasonable way to keep your work and progress in order. Believe me, in this game half the battle is organization, whether it be looking for half-a-dozen people simultaneously as I do, or simply trying to find an old aunt or uncle.

As a professional I also write daily reports on each of my active cases. These are then entered in the case file and seperated from the rest of the material contained therein. These neat and chronologically documented reports afford quick reference and mind refreshment. They also serve as a recap of my work to date for my clients and allows them to see my progress. The clients are satisfied, allowing me to spend my time where it's needed, investigating.

Something else I attach inside the case file is a form I call a SUBJECT INFORMATION SHEET, or **SUBJECT INFO SHEET** for short (see following page). You may duplicate this one or have your own made. This handy sheet is a ready source of information and is your checklist to success. First, fill in all of the blanks for which you already have information. (Most people are surprised how much information they already have accumulated). Use additional sheets as necessary. Now as you "develop" more information, fill in your subject info sheet. This one page allows a quick and ready reference at your fingertips. No need to go through an entire file for a phone number again. Some investigators have a form similar to this printed directly on the cover of their case file folders. It looks good but I do not like the idea of the whole world seeing this kind of information. A suggestion might be to have the subject info sheet printed on the inside of the jacket cover.

I use my subject info sheet religiously. In fact, in my office I use them as scratch pads near the phones. Can you see why? Get some made for yourself and use them.

SUBJECT:_____   CASE NO.: _____

ITEM	SOURCE	DATE	INFORMATION
Also known as (aka)			
Last known address			
Last known phone number			
Autos/Vehicles			
Known Police Record			
Birth Date			
Social Security Number			
Political Party			
Real Property Owned			
Driving History			
Driver's License Humber			
Credit History			
Educational History			
Employment History			
Family History			
Spouse's Name			
Children			
Relatives			
Neighbors			
Friends			
Hobby/Interests			
Medical History			
Maiden Name			
Height			
Weight			
Color Eyes/Hair			
Other			
Present Location			

12.0 CONCLUSION

Dear Reader:

My attempt with this book has been to present the information you need as clearly and to the point as possible. In doing so I have wasted no words or paper.... or any of your time. However as a result in several instances I have left much up to you. My hope is that I have created an awareness and a new sense of thinking. Because in order to be successful in this business one must be a thinker. And though you will find each case to be different, each successive case will be more like the rest. As your skills and experience grow, so will your condidence. But by only reading this book you will find no one. It will take action and hard work.

I often receive letters from readers who claim to have greatly enjoyed my book but ask me questions which clearly indicate they have done nothing in their individual searches. Some I suspect read only a chapter or two. They ask questions which are clearly answered in subsequent chapters. They have difficulty because they lack initiative. Without it you will not develop experience or confidence. Two very important elements I can not teach.

By now I hope you are motivated and anxious to begin. The methods and procedures you have read are precise and accurate, I assure you. And with action and hard work you will be successful. Get started today. It's an enjoyable business so have fun.

Good Hunting,

Eugene Ferraro

Eugene Ferraro

P.S. Should you have any questions or comments I welcome them. I answer all of my mail personally. Write:

TARGET BOOKS
Eugene Ferraro
407 West Santa Clara Avenue
Santa Ana, CA 92706

INDEX